MADAME PELE

PELE

TRUE ENCOUNTERS WITH
HAWAI'I'S FIRE GODDESS

Also by Rick Carroll

Great Outdoor Adventures of Hawaii
Hawai'i's Best Spooky Tales: The Original
Hawai'i's Best Spooky Tales
Hawai'i's Best Spooky Tales 2
Hawai'i's Best Spooky Tales 3
Hawai'i's Best Spooky Tales 4
Hawai'i's Best Spooky Tales 5
IZ: Voice of the People

with Marcie Carroll

Hawai'i: True Stories of the Island Spirit
The Unofficial Guide to Hawaii
The Unofficial Guide to Maui

MADAME PELE

TRUE ENCOUNTERS WITH HAWAI'I'S FIRE GODDESS

Including 14 stories published in the
Hawai'i's Best Spooky Tales series

COLLECTED BY RICK CARROLL

3565 Harding Ave.
Honolulu, Hawai'i 96816
www.besspress.com

Design: Carol Colbath

Library of Congress Cataloging-in-Publication Data

Carroll, Rick.
  Madame Pele: true encounters
with Hawaii's fire goddess /
collected by Rick Carroll.
     p. cm.
  ISBN 9781573061452
  1. Pele (Hawaiian deity).
2. Goddesses - Hawaii. 3. Mythology,
Hawaiian. 4. Legends - Hawaii.
I. Title.
GR510.C37 2003   299.92-dc21

Background photographs on pages 28–30, 59, 60, and 98–102 were taken by
scientists of the U.S. Geological Survey, U.S. Department of Interior.

For Paul Morris, M.D., the Honolulu surgeon at
The Queen's Medical Center who saved my life two
years ago

Contents

Hitchhiking

Pele's Rocks

ACKNOWLEDGMENTS

Some books appear in a dream, others evolve over time and space. This book surfaced as an idle thought while staring in awe at the volcano twenty years ago, and then, story by story, came to life, proving some books, like great wine, take time.

For Pele, who provided the inspiration, for Marcie and Shannon, who were there at the beginning, for the crew at Bess Press (Buddy, Revé, and Carol) who helped make my idea a reality, for all the many storytellers who continue to amaze me with their diverse backgrounds and varied experiences, and for all you who stay up late at night reading my books, I can only say, *mahalo*, over and again.

INTRODUCTION

"Enter not prayerless the house of Pele."
—Hawaiian chant

Join me, if you dare, on the raw, red, burning edge of Hawai'i, biggest island in the tropical Pacific, and I will tell you stories of Madame Pele, the most respected and feared deity in Polynesia.

True stories of creation and destruction, of hell-fire eruptions, and ancient armies lost, whole villages consumed by fire, and houses up in smoke.

Real stories about unfortunate souls who steal Pele's rocks, cavalier folks who ignore her, infidels who think she's fiction.

Be warned: The stories you are about to read are sworn accounts by people who have met Pele in spirit or the flesh.

Some survive Pele's Curse. Many doubt it. Those who do suffer a dreadful fate. Some come away believers.

Not just a wispy myth, Madame Pele is seen daylight or dusk in various forms on all inhabited Hawaiian Islands.

Beware the wrinkled crone in white (sometimes, red) gown; she can turn you to stone with a glance.

Be wary of young, beautiful women who beg a smoke.

Avoid, if you can, fireballs that rocket between volcanoes.

Be on the lookout for a little white dog that appears just before a volcanic eruption.

Old woman, young woman, fireball, little white dog—all are earthly manifestations of Hawai'i's fire goddess. Sometimes, she even appears as a man.

Whatever form she takes, Pele leaves folks ashen and trembling; she turns skeptics into mush.

Those who say they don't believe in "that old Hawaiian stuff" are most likely to encounter her fiery charms.

I must admit that for the longest time I remained skeptical about Pele's appearances—until I had a personal encounter on the Big Island in broad daylight one October on what turned out to be the hottest day of the year. What happened is revealed in "The Passenger," one of twenty-nine first-person, eye-witness accounts by contributing authors to this anthology.

Contributing authors include scientists, a university professor, a retired judge, journalists, local Hawaiians, *kama'āina* and visitors alike, all with one thing in common: an unforgettable Pele encounter.

Their stories curl your hair and shiver your bones, make you think twice about giving hitchhikers a lift after dark, or taking rocks from Hawai'i. (By the way: *Akamai* folks in Hawai'i know Pele's Curse is fiction invented years ago by a tour guide, yet hundreds of purloined rocks keep coming back to the Islands every year from luckless souls. Decide for yourself after reading their woeful tales.)

◈

"Pele is very much alive in Hawaii today."

—H. Arlo Nimmo, *The Pele Literature: An Annotated Bibliography of the English-Language Literature on Pele, Volcano Goddess of Hawaii.*

Nineteen eighty-three was a banner year for Madame Pele.

At 12:31 a.m. on January 23, Pele kicked off the longest-running show in the volcanic history of the Hawaiian Islands.

Since that day lava has erupted almost nonstop from Kīlauea volcano and shows no sign of abating.

The start of Pele's record tantrum coincided with the beginning of my time in the Islands. That year I took early retirement from the *San Francisco Chronicle*, sold my Stinson Beach shack, bought a one-way ticket to Hawai'i, and set off on an extended tour of Asia and the Pacific.

First stop: Hawai'i Volcanoes National Park, where I wanted to experience the fury of a live volcano; Hawai'i is the only place on the planet you can get safely up close to an eruption.

I visited the park at high noon on a voggy Good Friday with my wife, Marcie, and daughter, Shannon, and for some reason, probably the observance of the

Christian holy day, we were the only people in the park, or so it seemed.

We hiked Devastation Trail, marched across steaming Kīlauea Iki crater, stood on the edge of burbling Halemaʻumaʻu crater, probed drippy Thurston Lava Tube, and hiked beyond the end of Chain of Craters Road to see the red.

In 1870, Mark Twain visited the volcano and thought the fire and smoke reminded him of hell, but as I stood there surrounded by black lava covering red hot magma it all seemed to me somehow sacred, not like in a church full of statues, but sacred in a primal, supernatural way.

I felt the presence of an invisible power. More than once, I glanced over my shoulder to see if someone, Madame Pele, perhaps? was there. Nobody ever was.

Overwhelmed by the artistry and magnitude of Pele's work, I left the park a little disappointed, for I had hoped to have a personal encounter with the fire goddess herself. It was not to be, not then.

Shortly after that first visit, Pele sparked not one but two Big Island eruptions, and for the first time in 116 years Kīlauea and Mauna Loa erupted at the same time.

I returned to the Big Island as often as I could to get a close look at Pele's work in progress.

Nothing can prepare you for the awesome sight of a live volcano, one of the earth's great natural wonders, spewing fountains of fire into the sky. Or sending red hot molten lava right by your feet, your toes, on the race to the sea.

The sights and smells of creation and destruction amount to sensory overload and create in me an internal conflict of fear and fascination. I want to flee and stay there forever.

Over the next two decades, succumbing to what can only be described as Pele fever, I returned many times to the Big Island to admire the ever changing lavascape.

Whenever I could, I flew in helicopters over Kīlauea's yawning fire pit, peered into skylights that revealed rushing rivers of red-orange lava, and remembered the beauty of the lost village of Kalapana now entombed under tons of 'a'ā. I photographed Waha'ula Heiau from above before it, too, was smothered and sealed in perpetuity.

On three interisland voyages, I sailed by the burning shore aboard old steamships, and as often as possible, hiked at night across red-veined, fresh *pāhoehoe* lava with my sneakers smoking in early stages of meltdown.

I reread the earliest known Pele stories by the London missionary William Ellis in his 1827 journal, and those by Jack London's wife, Charmian, in her 1917 book, *Our Hawaii*. I especially enjoyed Armine von Tempski's vivid descriptions of Pele's power in her 1930 book, *Lava: A Saga of Hawaii*.

With great regularity Pele stories appear, usually on Page One, of every Hawai'i newspaper from Hilo to Hanalei; the earliest I found was in the 1917 *Pacific Commercial Advertiser*. My favorite, "Remembering The Time I Met Pele," was written by the late Pierre Bowman of the *Honolulu Star Bulletin* in 1984. The most recent was only last week.

Over the years, I clipped Pele tales from *Time* magazine, *Harpers*, the *New Yorker*, *National*

Geographic, and mainland newspapers. My colleague Stan Delaplane wrote about Pele's thirst for gin in the *San Francisco Chronicle*, James D. Houston wrote in the *San Francisco Examiner* about hard-luck victims who return Pele's rocks to Hawai'i Volcanoes National Park rangers. On visits home Annie Nakao wrote stories about Pele encounters for both San Francisco papers.

Soon I came to know otherwise God-fearing folks who claimed to have seen Madame Pele recently in one form or another in the Islands.

Ex-journalist and author Gordon Morse swore he and two witnesses ran into Madame Pele on the Big Island in broad daylight one afternoon.

Schoolteacher Helen Fujie recalled that her husband Roy met Pele on Lāna'i years ago.

Akoni Akana described a strange and eerie force that descended like a fog on his Maui *hula hālau* while they were visiting Laka's hula platform, a known Pele site, on the island of Kaua'i.

Hawai'i storyteller Nyla Fujii told me about the mischief Pele caused her and fellow storyteller Woody Fern one night in the village of Volcano.

I met a Castle Hospital nurse who told me her husband, a Kailua policeman, often sees Pele thumbing rides in Waimānalo.

My neighbor Michael Dalke had an exasperating encounter with a client who pocketed rocks one night on Chain of Craters Road.

Were they all pulling my leg? I don't think so. People don't make up stories like these. One look in their eyes and I could tell something out of the ordinary had occurred.

Pele encounters, it began to occur to me, were not episodes that occurred long ago in the misty past; they were happening right now!

Soon I had in hand a growing body of evidence that Madame Pele is not a figment of imagination, not just a long ago legend or myth, not a fictional character at all, but a contemporary spirit in the Hawaiian Islands today, a force and a power as real as the volcano itself.

After reviewing more than one hundred Pele stories from the early 1800s to the day before yesterday, I selected a few of my favorites.

For your late night reading pleasure, I am proud to present the first anthology of *Madame Pele: True Encounters with Hawai'i's Fire Goddess*. If you run into Madame Pele hitchhiking on Chain of Craters Road, or anywhere in the Islands today, just say aloha, give her a lift, and, please, let me know what happens next.

"Step lightly, for you are on holy ground,"
—Hawaiian caveat

Spirit, legend, or reality? It is up to you to decide.

Whatever conclusion you reach, one thing is certain: You cannot fail to wonder at Madame Pele and her faithful followers who respect and worship her, and continue to delight in her caprice.

And in the larger sense, isn't that all of us?

Now, the goddess awaits.
Offer a ti leaf, say a prayer.
Come, enter the realm of Pele.

Rick Carroll
Volcano, Hawai'i

ON THE
BIG ISLAND

2

The Lady in the Crimson Dress

Barbara Swift

This story takes place at Volcano House. It involves my number-two daughter, Maile. We first took her to the Big Island when she was about four years old. (I'm the mainland *haole* and my husband is the Hawaiian from Maui.) We spent Thanksgiving on the Hilo side and did the usual tourist thing.

One of our excursions was to Volcano House and Chain of Craters Road. We wanted to see the volcano and the work of Madame Pele.

We went to the lookout at Volcano House to see the caldera. Maile was running around, going up and down the little hill. Our family was standing by the lava rock wall when Maile came running down the hill from the hotel. I picked her up and stood her on the wall so that she could see.

She started waving, and I asked what she was waving at. Well, my four-year-old looked at me and said: "The lady in the crimson dress." She was waving at the lady in the crimson dress, Madame Pele.

Now if you know four-year-olds, you know that just identifying the color red can be a challenge for them. A smart four-year-old knows the color red, but not crimson. The word "crimson" is not in their vocabulary. It was certainly not in Maile's. It's not a word in common use in our home, either.

She had seen Pele. The rest of us saw absolutely nothing, not even a puff of smoke. She stood and stared, looking again for the lady in the crimson dress.

We took her back to the Big Island and the Volcano House when she was older. We went around to the lookout at the caldera. Maile went quickly out to the edge as far as she could go. A small white fence had been put up because of a crack in the earth near the edge.

My daughter started to cry and held onto the fence saying, "Does she know that I am here? I have many sisters."

I was filming this incident, but had to turn the camera off and pry her hands off the fence. There were several people there and they were all staring.

After our return home to O'ahu, for a long time she would occasionally carry small lava rocks around in her hands, sometimes wetting them. Often she would say, "The lava has to be wet." She would then turn the water on and wet the rocks.

We haven't been back to the Big Island since she became an adult. She remembers all of this but really doesn't talk about it.

I feel that when she does go back that she shouldn't go alone.

Pele

Gordon Morse

The day we met Pele we were not supposed to meet anyone. Please note the "we." There were three witnesses to this story of meeting the fiery goddess of Hawai'i volcanoes. I wouldn't dare tell you about this if I had been alone.

My friends were a pilot, a scientist, and a sugar plantation manager.

Our visit with Pele was in the spring of 1955. The goddess was island building down in the lower Puna area on the flank of Kīlauea Volcano. It was the first eruption in modern history to happen in a populated area.

For over a week a large section of Puna had been cut off from the rest of the island by two rivers of molten lava as they raced from the vents into the ocean. Residents of the area were now refugees in a school gymnasium in the sugar town of Pāhoa.

The manager of the Puna Sugar Company wanted to inspect what was left of his fields in the abandoned area. He talked the pilot of a small plane into landing on a cinder road between the lava flows so he could inspect the area on foot.

Since there were two empty seats in the airplane, a volcano scientist was invited to go along. I was talked into going to record the trip with camera and pen as I was a newsman in those days.

The pilot landed the Cessna aircraft on the road. The landing distance was so short he had to stand on the brakes to keep from going into the bushes.

The four of us walked around inspecting the sugar fields, a path of bananas, and a sweet potato farm plot. There were no houses in this section.

Imagine our surprise when we came upon a Lady sitting at the edge of a sugar field.

Later I checked my notes and I definitely wrote her down as a Lady. That's the impression I had. In my estimation, a girl would have been under twenty. She was older, but not by much.

If it were a woman, the person would have showed more maturity in dress and hairdo, and a certain domestication of mannerisms. You know, she would have had that look that sends children to bed without a fuss at eight p.m.

But a Lady has the charm of sophistication. She carries herself with authority even when sitting. She has soft features, clearness of skin, a sculpturing of the nose that denotes breeding. This Lady sitting by the side of the path had all of these at first glance.

She wore a red *mu'umu'u* with black markings that resembled bamboo. She displayed no jewelry. A cloud of jet black hair flowed behind her shoulders and down to the middle of her back. She was barefoot.

"Hi," said the manager, recovering from his surprise.

"Aloha," she answered.

To this day I cannot truthfully explain how that "aloha" sounded. Something like a lover saying it to his love in the moonlight with the sound of the sea whispering on sands would be a fair attempt.

"What are you doing here?" asked the sugar planter in an authoritative voice. After all, he owned this land.

"Just resting in the shade of the sugarcane," the lady replied, giving us a radiant smile.

"No one is supposed to be in this area," the scientist said. "The National Guard evacuated everyone a week ago. Why did you stay behind? You know you're trapped in between lava flows here."

The Lady's smile just grew wider as if that were answer enough.

"What's your name?" I inquired, poising a pencil over my notebook.

She said something very musical in Hawaiian that sounded to me like the name of a fern. I wrote it down phonetically, and it appears as "u'ulei" in my notes. (Later, I looked the word up in a Hawaiian dictionary. It's actually 'ūlei, a Hawai'i shrub with small white rose-like flowers.)

The pilot frowned and turned to us. "I could make two trips in the plane and take her out," he said.

"Oh, I won't leave here," the Lady said. "At least not today. I have work to do. Perhaps I'll be ready to go somewhere else next week."

"Well, if you don't want to come away with us

now, you may have to later today or tomorrow," the scientist said. "We'll have to report you to Civil Defense and they will send a helicopter in for you. The eruption has caused an emergency in this part of the island, and there are laws to protect people."

"I follow my own laws," the Lady said, and for the first time she stopped smiling.

I remember looking into her eyes at that moment and what I saw was familiar. While in college, I had spent a Christmas vacation with some friends in a home on a frozen lake in Wisconsin. We all slept in the living room because the cast iron stove could only heat that room. The stove was loaded with wood at bedtime, but by dawn it was freezing to the touch. However, when I lifted the lid to put in more wood, there were two gleaming cherry-red coals nestling in the gray ashes that promised instant rekindling.

The Lady's features were now cold, and those same two glowing coals were deep within her gray eyes.

Perhaps my three companions had somewhat the same feeling, because the manager said, "We'll finish our inspection of this area, and if you want to go out with us, you can wait by the plane." He gestured up the road toward where we landed.

We continued walking. But for some strange reason, we had only gone ten feet or so when the idea that this might be Pele entered our minds simultaneously. We turned around to again look at the Lady.

She was gone!

We ran back. The manager plunged into the cane field. The pilot went up the road. The scientist jogged down another path. I stood and called her name. We didn't find her.

A spooky feeling began to creep into all of us, like a cloud invading a rain forest at dusk.

"I think it's time to go," the pilot said.

No one disagreed.

We got into the plane and taxied to the end of the cinder road. The pilot gunned the engine and stood on the brakes. When he released the brakes, we lurched forward. Halfway down the road it was obvious the plane was too heavily loaded to clear the trees ahead. Landing on a small road was one thing. Taking off with a heavy load was another.

We stopped.

"Someone has to get out," the pilot said. "I'll come back for you later."

The "you" was directed at me. I was sitting next to the door. For reasons not entirely clear to me, I made no protest and got out of the plane.

I was scared. I did not want to socialize with anyone, especially a Lady. And as the plane took off, diminished to a dot, then disappeared, I fervently wished I was somewhere else. Anywhere else would do.

My thoughts were of Pele sightings I had read. They were usually about seeing an old woman, or a pretty young one, during an eruption.

The common one is that she is hitchhiking, gets into a car, asks for a cigarette, lights it with the tip of her finger, and then, when the driver momentarily looks the other way, she disappears.

Another story is that she comes to a house accompanied by a white dog and asks for something to eat or drink. When given something, she goes on her way. But if she is refused, she stamps her foot, and very soon a finger of molten lava branches off from the main flow and destroys the house.

An hour dragged by, and when no Lady appeared, I began to laugh at myself. That wasn't Pele. She was probably a resident who had decided to stay in the area to take care of her cat or dog. I had a name and description.

I would solve this mystery once I got out.

The pilot did return, and an hour later I walked into Civil Defense headquarters at the refugee gym. The pilot, the scientist, and the sugar planter were there. The four of us grilled the residents of Puna. The Lady's name and description didn't fit anyone they knew. The National Guard commander and Civil Defense workers all assured us they had done a thorough job in getting everyone out—people and their pets.

I Saw Madame Pele, in Person

Julieta P. Cobb

When I came to the United States in the spring of 1991 from the Philippines, I knew nothing about Hawai'i lore. I had never heard of Madame Pele.

In early 1992 my husband, Dwight, and I went to the Big Island for a visit and to do some sightseeing. We spent the night in Hilo, and early in the morning we drove up to Volcanoes National Park. It was still early when we got there, so we decided to go to Volcano House hotel and restaurant for breakfast.

We were the first ones to eat, and when we finished eating I told my husband that I wanted to use the restroom. I went down a hallway from the dining room to the restroom. I entered the restroom and proceeded to a stall.

When I finished, I opened the door to the stall and saw a tall woman with long black hair and a long white dress standing by the sink. I had not heard her come in.

She did not speak to me, so I did not speak to her.

I washed my hands and left. She was there the entire time, but didn't move—to go to a stall or wash her hands or anything. She just stood there without moving.

When I left the restroom, I saw my husband standing in the main hallway. I went to him and asked if he had seen a tall Hawaiian woman go into the restroom. He told me nobody had gone into the restroom; she would have had to pass him to get there.

Just then I turned and saw a large picture on the wall. It was a picture of the lady I had seen in the restroom.

"There she is right there," I told my husband. "Is she the owner of this hotel or something?"

He told me, "That's Madame Pele, the Hawaiian goddess of the volcano, not a real person."

When I told him I had just seen that lady in the restroom, he told me that was impossible. He was laughing at me, and I was getting angry with him because I knew what I had seen.

About that time a Korean lady who was opening the gift shop overheard us talking. She came over and asked me what I had seen. I told her that I had seen the tall woman in the picture in the restroom, but that my husband wouldn't believe me.

She did not laugh at me. She told me this had happened before with people who are attuned to it.

Since this incident, I have read a lot about Madame Pele. But I don't care what I read or what people say. On that morning in that hotel restroom I saw Madame Pele in person.

At the Volcano's Edge

Nyla Fujii-Babb

Christmas, 1988. My friend and fellow Native Hawaiian storyteller, Woody Fern, and I were invited by the Volcano Art Center to do two storytelling performances at the Hawai'i Volcanoes National Park.

We took an early flight to Hilo, checked in at Uncle Billy's Hilo Bay Hotel, and proceeded in our brand new subcompact rental car to the park, some twenty-five miles out of Hilo town. Our road led through what was once the great Pana'ewa Forest. Out of respect for the "Lady," Woody and I had both agreed that we would not tell traditional legends about Pele; rather, we would tell stories of Hawai'i's history and stories of Pele's sister, Hi'iaka, who had battled the *mo'o* Pana'ewa somewhere in these forested regions.

Our first performance was to take place in the morning at an overlook near the crater's rim. Seated with the rim at our backs, we told stories of Princess

Ruth, Hiʻiaka and Panaʻewa, Big Island sharks, Robert Louis Stevenson in Hawaiʻi, and many others to fifteen or twenty park visitors. The sky was clear, and everything seemed peaceful. We returned to Hilo to rest, shower, and have dinner.

That evening Woody and I were to return to do a Christmas program at the Kīlauea Military Camp Theatre for guests of an Elderhostel tour. The program would begin at 7:30 that evening. At 6:30 it was already quite dark as we drove back toward the volcano. As we traveled along the highway through a stretch of the old Panaʻewa Forest, suddenly the car engine began to sputter and the car stalled several times before surging to life again. Perhaps it was a portent, but the rest of the ride was uneventful, though our minds were filled with unspoken thoughts.

That evening we told Christmas stories and pidgin English stories to a delighted group of a hundred. After the program was over, we were making our way back to the car in the parking lot when I noticed that I was missing the earring from my left ear. I had borrowed that earring from my daughter especially for this performance. It was silver and had been purchased from an art museum on the mainland as a gift for her. I was sure I had had the earring on at the beginning of the performance.

Our host and Woody accompanied an embarrassed me back to the theater, where we searched the stage and everywhere else I had been that evening. Having no luck, we returned to the car, where I ran my hands over every inch of the car's seats, between the seats, along the floors, and even in the paneling of the doors. The earring was NOT there!

Woody was quite concerned and offered to take out his mini mag-flashlight and help me search. The flashlight was in a briefcase that looked like a zippered pouch about ten inches by fifteen inches. Woody unzipped the case and felt inside for the flashlight. He couldn't find it. He turned his briefcase upside down and emptied the contents on the car seat. There were his pens, papers, and pencils, but no flashlight!

We returned to the hotel that evening, and I dreaded telling my daughter about her lost earring. Woody had emptied his briefcase once more back in his hotel room and searched his luggage for the flashlight—but it had simply disappeared! As I returned to my room, I said a little prayer that we would find these lost items and asked forgiveness if we had offended.

The next morning we packed and met in the lobby to catch the flight back to Honolulu. We carried our luggage out to the car in the parking lot. While Woody stowed the luggage in the trunk, I went to unlock the doors. There, right in the middle of the passenger-side seat, as if laid out for me to find, was the silver earring, glinting in the light of the early morning sun. It hadn't been there the night before.

I knew how thoroughly I had searched. I had run my hands over every inch of that seat searching for that earring. Now here it was twenty-five miles away from the place where I had lost it! How had it come to be placed in a locked car, twenty-five miles away, on the following morning? It was mystifying. I said a quiet "Mahalo" and we drove to the airport.

I had felt so bad about Woody losing his mag-flashlight, I told my husband when I got home that we would have to buy Woody another one. A few days later, however, Woody called. He had opened his briefcase at home and out fell his flashlight. Had it been there all that time—or had it just been returned?

Perhaps we should have given the "Lady" her due and told HER stories at the crater's rim—HER home. We do not know. Was it a warning or was it only a playful prank to remind these two modern storytellers that the old stories and the ancient places still have *mana*?

Weird Things Happen in Pele Land

Ted Timboy

I was born on O'ahu but grew up in Kona on the Big Island of Hawai'i. My mother comes from a family of coffee plantation people, and my dad grew up in the farming communities of the Islands.

Like most contemporary locals, I was raised with the stories and beliefs of the preceding generations that populated the islands. While I may not necessarily believe in wak-waks or ghost dogs, or even Madame Pele, there are some things that I follow "just because." I would never have meat in my car when I drive along Saddle Road, and I wouldn't dream of removing lava rocks from the Islands.

My boyfriend, Timm, and I were visiting Kona to celebrate my parents' fiftieth wedding anniversary as well as to enjoy an impromptu family reunion. While I had visited O'ahu numerous times since moving to California, my return to the Big Island came after nearly twenty years away. I've been living in San Francisco since 1986, and was looking forward to returning to the place where I grew up.

It was Timm's first trip to Hawai'i. Timm is a great traveling companion because he thoroughly researches any place he visits. Whether it's the cathedrals of the United Kingdom or the islands of Greece, Timm reads up on all aspects of the culture he will be visiting. He also brings a healthy respect for the land and people of any place where he will be a *malihini*, visitor.

Exploring Kona was wonderful. We had written up an itinerary of "must do's" that included seeing the volcano that had started erupting right before we left California. Our itinerary scheduled two days in which we'd view some petroglyphs then drive *mauka* through Waimea, continuing on to Laupāhoehoe and 'Akaka Falls, and finally to Hilo, where we would spend the night with my parents. We were then planning on viewing Madame Pele's lava flows at Volcano in the late evening before returning to Kona by the southerly Ka'ū route.

Timm wanted to visit the petroglyphs on the grounds of Mauna Lani Resort north of the Kona airport. Purported to be one of the largest surviving petroglyph fields in the Islands, the site is incredible. The guidebook suggested that the best times to view a petroglyph field were either early in the morning or late in the afternoon: this would allow the shadows to make the reliefs clearer for viewing and photographing.

We arrived at Mauna Lani a little after 7:00 a.m. and parked our rental car in the lot at the entrance to the viewing field. Because it was so early, Timm and I were the only people there.

Upon first entering the area that would lead us to the large field, we studied recreated petroglyphs on view for those who want to see these images up close and clearly defined.

Timm made sure to stop and read all the markers and take the time to study the sites and trails before us. The trail winds through about a quarter mile of *kiawe* forest and leads up to the petroglyph field. It took us about tewnty-five minutes to walk through the *kiawe* trees, and then we spent about ninety minutes studying and photographing the images.

After about two hours, we left the viewing field and began to follow the trail back to the parking lot. As we entered the *kiawe* forest, we talked about how spooky the location was and how neither one of us would want to be there after dark. As we followed the path, we heard the distinct sound of something heavy being pounded. The noise was very clear and timed like a metronome.

At first we thought that some workers were installing a new marker or chopping tree limbs, but we didn't see anyone. As we turned a corner in the path, we did see that a very old and heavy *kiawe* branch was rhythmically pounding itself against a slab of *pāhoehoe* stone. It didn't seem windy enough to cause just this one branch to move this way so I jokingly suggested that perhaps some spirits were in the woods with us then.

Shaking off the slight feeling of uneasiness, we continued along the path, expecting to be in the parking lot at the next turn, and instead came to a complete dead end! Timm supposed that we had stepped off the main path and onto a side trail used by employees, so we turned to retrace our steps back up the trail.

As we did so, we saw in front of us several dried flower *lei* hanging from the low branches of a tree. We studied the *lei* for a few minutes before once again determining to get back to the main trail. Just then a tourist family came walking up beside us.

I was about to tell them that we were all on a side trail when they simply smiled at us and continued on out into the main parking area! I swear that the trail had come to a dead end when we walked it.

Both Timm and I were stunned to see all this, but were in for a bigger shock when we realized that the dried *lei* were hanging directly over one of the markers we had stopped and read on the way into the viewing field!

The flowers were several days old, and there would have been no reason for anyone to hang them on the tree limbs during the two hours we were at the site.

We continued on uneventfully, taking the northern Waimea route to Hilo, arriving in Hilo late in the afternoon. After dinner, we drove to my folks' home right outside Hilo and I discovered that my older sister Marcia and her daughter Emma were also staying there.

As we settled down for an evening of talk story, I told my family about the strange events at Puakō. My sister said she had chicken skin, and my mom just looked at my dad and said, "You know who was doing that, right, honey?"

Marcia told us how she and Emma had gone out

to view Madame Pele's eruption the night before. She told us how clear the night was and how absolutely beautiful the lava flows had been. I told Timm that we should rest a bit then perhaps head out to the Volcano sometime after midnight to avoid the crowds.

No lie: just as I mentioned to Timm that we'd go to the crater later that night, the skies opened up and sheets of water came raining down all over Hilo. We had a laugh over the circumstances, and Timm said that maybe we should put off the visit to the crater until the next day! After more talk story we finally turned in for the evening.

Around 3:30 a.m., my dad woke us up with his knocking at the room door. I asked him if anything was wrong, and he said he just wanted to see if we were leaving for the volcano since the rental car headlights were on. Both Timm and I were pretty upset, thinking that we had left the lights on and that the car's battery would probably be drained.

Going outside with the car keys, we could see that the headlights were on with the light beams pointing into my parents' yard. Timm turned the headlights off and then tried turning the motor on. It revved to life with no hesitation.

Suddenly, the interior car lights began blinking on and off. Thinking that Timm was checking the light system, I knocked on the window and asked him if there were any other problems. Timm said that he hadn't even touched the interior lights; they had gone on and off by themselves.

Even stranger, there was about an inch of water on the floor of the driver's side of the car even though the rest of the car's interior was bone dry! The seats and all other areas of the floor in the car were dry, with the exception of the puddle near the gas and brake pedals. The car was parked on the level surface of my parents' front yard.

Rationalizing that the car might have suffered a short during the rainstorm, we decided the best course of action would be to swap the rental car for another car in the morning. We went back to bed and had a restless night.

Next day, we left my parents' house at about 7:30 a.m. and headed to the Hilo airport to exchange the car and proceed to Hawai'i Volcanoes National Park.

Anyone who has been there knows how eerie the drive into the park can be, especially when there is a heavy mist in the air. Timm mentioned that it was probably a good idea that we didn't go to view the eruption the night before, as the weather and narrow roads made the drive rather dangerous.

At the park, we went to the main visitors pavilion and watched the introductory video explaining how volcanoes work. We both enjoyed the fact that the video also went into some detail regarding the cultural aspects and importance of the volcanoes to the original settlers of the islands.

While wandering around the pavilion, I suddenly began to experience an awful headache. Not wanting to cut short Timm's first visit to this region, I told Timm that I would relax in the car and encouraged him to take his time exploring the park.

We drove to several of the usual sites around the park (the Volcano House, steam vents, and craters) and Timm walked around on his own taking photos while I tried to will my headache away. I fell into a deep sleep whenever Timm left to venture off on his own.

After several hours, Timm was hungry and suggested that I should get something into my stomach as I hadn't eaten anything the entire day. We drove out of the park and headed to Volcano town where we stopped by a little diner called the Lava Rock Cafe for lunch. The restaurant is a cute little eatery that filled up rather quickly with tourists as we sat at our table.

Like most local boys, I love to eat, but I was still feeling out of sorts and only ate half of my lunch before I went back to the car to get another nap. I was awakened by the car door opening, and Timm asked me if I wanted to get some fresh air. We walked around a bit, admiring the tropical plants and the beauty of the region, and Timm said that after I left to take a nap, he had gotten into a conversation with some of the tourists.

It seems that almost everyone had gone to view the eruption the night before, but it had turned into a fiasco: hundreds of people were wandering around the site, and many were lost. In the torrential rain many people panicked and lost their way off the paths or dropped and broke their flashlights. So many people were getting hurt that the park rangers had to set up a triage tent in the parking lot to treat people as they came out the Chain of Craters Road.

One of the tourists showed Timm a nasty scrape that extended from his ankle all the way up his thigh. His parting words to Timm were, "It's a good thing you didn't try to see the eruption last night; no one saw anything!" It seems that the rain coupled with heavy mist and steam from the craters ended up totally obscuring the lava flows that night. We never got to see Madame Pele's lava eruption but we had, indeed, been spared a disastrous trip!

One other strange thing happened. We left the Volcano area and drove down south through the Ka'ū desert with me still drifting in and out of sleep.

As soon as we left the Volcano area and hit Nā'ālehu (where my mom grew up), I suddenly was wide awake and hungry, with no headache!

Lady in Red

Lana T. Paiva

Have you ever heard about the Lady in Red? I have—many times as a young girl growing up on the Big Island. My older sister, Hazel, worked at Hertz car rental. She would tell me the volcano would soon erupt because the Lady in Red was seen arriving at the Hilo Airport via Hawaiian Airlines and hailing a cab to take that beautiful drive to the Hawai'i Volcanoes National Park to pay her respects to Madame Pele. I'd never seen her—until 1986.

One beautiful afternoon, my husband, Wendell, and I decided to take a ride up to the park. I had packed a picnic dinner of musubi, fried chicken, egg roll, vienna sausage, and kim chee. At around 6:00 p.m., as we were cruising along the Chain of Craters Road, we decided to park along the Nāpau Crater. We were alone, enjoying the cool, crisp, gentle breezes, ready to eat our dinner, when a taxi drove up and parked in front of us. Who do you think got out? It was the Lady in Red!

She strolled across the parking lot, crossed the Chain of Craters Road, and stood at the foot of a row of old spatter cones. No visible steam rose from any of the cones. The Lady in Red chanted in Hawaiian and tossed in some coins. The vents roared to life with steam!

As the taxi driver waited to take her to her next destination, Wendell and I looked at each other in disbelief. We decided to leave the area immediately! Would the earth start to tremble? Would the road split open and make it impossible for us to leave? Where did the Lady in Red come from? Where did she go? Who was she? We still don't know.

Death of Waha'ula Heiau

Rick Carroll

Aloha, Waha'ula, hello, good-bye. Nothing is sacred. Madame Pele gives and she takes away.

Take Waha'ula Heiau on the Big Island of Hawai'i. Built in A.D. 1250, the stone temple of Waha'ula is one of the bloodiest sacrificial *heiau* in all of Hawai'i (its name means "red or sore mouth").

Waha'ula was the last temple abandoned by chiefs who banned ancient rites just before Christian missionaries arrived in 1820. A century later, the stones of Waha'ula still held enough power to claim a young man's life at the Bishop Museum; he fell and smashed his skull on a *heiau* made of its rocks. Those rocks, I hope to tell you, had *mana*.

Four times since 1989, lava rolled right up to the *heiau* and stopped. Never entered, stopped cold, outside the front door. Which is pretty spooky when you stop to think about it.

Some folks said you could look at this as a kind of primal power play. The *heiau* had—as it had done for centuries—defeated Madame Pele by standing fast against her fiery breath. Still others said Madame Pele paused out of respect for the *heiau*.

Either way, Waha'ula stood inviolate, a hardy survivor on the Big Island's volcano coast, unlike two hundred houses in the once picturesque village of Kalapana, historic fishing villages and canoe landings, and the park's $1.2 million visitors' center—all gone, consumed by fire, smothered under red hot lava.

In 1997, something awful happened that shook everyone's belief. Waha'ula Heiau was overrun by lava. The oldest and one of the most sacred *heiau* in Hawai'i was gone, inundated by tons of molten lava.

The death of Waha'ula shocked folks at Hawai'i Volcanoes National Park. People couldn't believe their eyes. The Hilo newspaper called the loss "devastating."

Local residents "stood in silence and awe," the Associated Press said, "as lava engulfed the temple, leaving only the top of its five-foot-high stone walls visible, and flowed into the Pacific Ocean."

Once lava spilled over the walls, the *heiau* filled like an overflowing bathtub, an eyewitness said. "It's just gone, completely gone. We never thought it would go that quickly," said a shaken Mardie Lane, Hawai'i Volcanoes National Park spokesperson. "Waha'ula has withstood so much over the years it just didn't enter our consciousness that it would go so fast." The nearby priest's house was buried in ten minutes.

For eight hundred years, many islanders believed Madame Pele, the goddess of volcanoes, had spared the temple. Had the *heiau* lost its power over Madame Pele? Are there limits to power in the supernatural? Or did Madame Pele, known to be fractious, lose her temper? Was it something someone said or did?

Wave a ti leaf, toss salt, look for signs. The answer is on the wind. All anybody knows for sure is this: Nothing's sacred now, not even a most sacred *heiau*.

I thought of Madame Pele and Waha'ula the other day when Big Island Mayor Harry Kim reopened a section of lava-covered Chain of Craters Road and started charging tourists five dollars to see Madame Pele's latest work in progress. That didn't seem very aloha-like. I knew sooner or later something would happen. You knew it, too. A week after the grand opening of Chain of Craters Road, Madame Pele sent a fresh river of lava spilling eight miles down the slopes of Kīlauea Volcano. The lava smothered Harry Kim's new road. Nothing's sacred.

Don't look now, but isn't that Madame Pele dancing on Kīlauea's east rift zone?

Pele Dream

Pua Lilia (Elise) DuFour

The day was bright; the sky was full of vog washing the sky gray. The air smelled thick and had a sense of foreboding to it. Birds were unusually absent and there wasn't a wisp of wind. Towering palm trees stood like sentinels watching over the sparse landscape, protecting it, holding it against the ferocious winds that can whip across the land at times. The sea glistened a brilliant turquoise, contrasting with the gray sky.

I found myself walking down a rock path toward a village. As I walked along, the sky began to darken ahead of me. Nearing the village I came upon an old woman sitting along the side of the road. She was bent and decrepit with stringy white hair. Wearing dirty rags, she looked like a beggar. There was something about her that gave me chills up the back of my neck. When I got closer, she looked up at me and asked for a drink and a cigarette. Her eyes were the color of coal.

I told her I didn't have anything on me, but if she accompanied me to the nearby village we could get her some water and probably find her a cigarette. She thanked me. I helped her up. She put her arm in mine. We began a slow walk to the village.

Nearing the village, we began encountering people. The old woman asked each one she passed for a drink and a cigarette. She was met with derisive comments, pushed aside, and laughed at. Each time, she put her head down and muttered something under her breath. Then she'd turn back to me, take my arm, and we'd continue on toward the village.

Once inside the village we headed toward the well in the center of the square. The farther into the village we went, the more villagers stared, laughed and made rude comments toward the old woman. I felt angry and embarrassed for her. Once I tried to protect her. She reached out, took hold of my arm, and told me to keep my voice, that soon she would have her day.

When we reached the well, I got a drink of water for her first. As soon as she drank, I turned to get one for myself. As I drank, a hush fell around the square. I turned, and suddenly the old woman was gone and in her place was a tall beautiful woman with fire in her eyes, coal black wavy hair, and a foreboding frown. I knew this must be Pele. But how? What happened to the old woman?

She looked down at me, smiled, and touched my cheek, knowing my wonder. Then she turned toward the villagers and her voice sounded like thunder: "You ignored me and laughed at me. For that you will be punished." The villagers suddenly knew she was Pele, the goddess of fire, and rushed forward to kneel and beg forgiveness.

Ignoring them, she turned back to me and said, "Leave here quickly and never look back. There is a rocky knoll a short distance down the trail from here. Go there and wait. You will be safe there. Do not look back to this village as you leave or you will suffer the same as they do."

With that she vanished.

The people in the square began crying and wailing in panic. Suddenly they were running everywhere, trying to flee before Pele took her revenge. I left quickly.

As I was leaving, a loud rumbling began behind me. It grew louder and the ground began to shake violently. It sounded like thousands of freight trains rumbling toward me. I wanted to turn and look, but remembered her warning and began to run. I could feel intense heat behind me and knew Pele was exacting her revenge with fire. I saw the rocky knoll and headed for it.

As soon I reached the knoll, lava suddenly was all around me. I started to cry, afraid I would be dead within seconds. I raised my arms, closed my eyes, and pleaded with Pele to spare my life. Suddenly I was calm; I felt protected and knew I was safe and would live to see the sunset that day.

I don't know how long I stood with my arms outstretched. When I opened my eyes, I looked around and found I was alone in a sea of black lava. Everything was gone—the village, the people, trees; there was no sign of any life around me. Everything was wiped clean. It had become deathly quiet. Life had ceased to exist on this small spot of the world. Not even the wind dared raise his voice to the anger of Pele. The sun began to set, and the sky became a glowing orange-red. Watching the day end, I was suddenly at peace. Something amazing had happened, and somehow I was a part of it.

I watched the sun turn to cinders as it slipped over the horizon. I lost track of time and lay down to rest. I must have slept, because suddenly I felt something wet and cold across my face. I opened my eyes, wiped my hand across my wet face and looked up at a huge black dog standing over me. Around his neck was a golden flask. He licked me again as I sat up. The eyes of this dog were sea green and sparkled with flecks of gold that glinted in the light. It was as though you could fall into the depths of his eyes when you looked deep enough. This was the largest dog I'd ever seen, towering over me by several feet. When I got up, he nudged me and rubbed his neck against me.

I untied the flask, opened it, and smelled the contents. A sweet fragrance came to my nose. I knew it was safe. When I began to drink a voice came to me. "For your generosity and kindness I repay you with my drink. I have spared you and sent my devoted dog to aid you in your journey home. He is faithful and will lead you to safety. Heed him well, for he is my favorite. Thank you for all you've done and will do. You are in my favor."

I drained the flask and felt refreshed. As I looked at the dog, his eyes began to glow, and he looked toward the horizon where the sun had set. I suddenly knew how to get home.

I stepped from the knoll to walk in the direction he had gazed. When I turned to see if he was following me, he was gone. I was alone once again, but I knew where I needed to be. As I started on my journey home, the horizon started to glow purple from dawn approaching.

I rolled over and woke up. I was sweating, and my hair was matted against the back of my neck. Whew! What a dream!

Later that day, I discussed this dream with Auntie Dalina. She hugged me long and smiled. "You have been blessed, Pua; use it for the lesson it is and remember, you are now Hawai'i's child."

One Night on the Volcano Coast

Walt Wrzesniewski

My wife Janine and I introduced our friend Barbara from Connecticut to Madame Pele's home. We hiked out in the late afternoon, enjoyed the sunset, and were awed by the lava flowing down a hillside—and especially by the lava spewing into the sea.

Getting back to the car parked at the end of Chain of Craters Road, however, was quite an adventure.

I had memorized a set of stars to guide us back, and we had flashlights, but it still took Janine, Barbara, and me twice as long to get back as it did to get out there. Along the way back, we got worried when we heard the surf—too, too close on our left.

Shining our flashlights up, we saw a sign high on a ridge to our right. It was the sign that begged hikers not to go beyond the point where we now were because of the danger of shelves collapsing into the rugged surf, an almost guaranteed death.

We managed to get ourselves to less treacherous ground and back on course. Despite the danger all along the way, though, we felt a sense of goodwill—of warmth and guidance.

All three of us are members of the ECKANKAR clergy. As such, we have a deep respect for the beliefs of others. We also, through our spiritual exercises, have learned to see and hear with our "inner" senses.

So no one was surprised when we started seeing eyes glowing in the darkness out there on the lava field.

We saw one or more sets of eyes, kind of glowing and floating just several feet away. It seemed as if someone sent us an escort.

Even though this is a "spooky" tale, I want to underscore the fact that Barbara, Janine, and I felt nothing but benevolence. After our trek and the close call by the ocean ledge, we were very happy for the company of entities who knew the way. They certainly had a presence.

And, once, in my peripheral vision, I saw the whole person, not just the eyes. I saw a Polynesian man, short in stature, mostly naked, who seemed both curious and filled with caring and concern for our welfare. He wasn't smiling, but his face glowed with goodwill.

Now that we felt safe, the three of us sort of just "knew" the path back. I don't know if our friends were guiding us telepathically, but we found our way straight to the end of Chain of Craters Road and our parked car. We never made a wrong turn again.

We extended our gratitude to God and all of the servants of the Spirit of God. As ECKists, we believe God loves us so much, the Spirit of God will take whatever shape or form is necessary to help us. As such, Madame Pele and any other gods, demigods, or other entities are just as real as necessary for the experience of that particular Soul.

Barbara, Janine, and I have a deep love and respect for Hawai'i and all who live and have lived here; so, it's natural to have a love and respect for Pele.

In fact, when we lived on the mainland, Janine and I once brought home black sand and lava rocks. Later, we heard all the stories of bad luck. But we had nothing but good luck and love. We think it's because our attitude was one of respect. They weren't souvenirs; we just wanted a piece of the *'āina* for our deep connection over many lifetimes with Hawai'i.

Getting back to the story: Barbara, Janine, and I got into our rental car physically exhausted but spiritually invigorated. We began the twenty-mile drive back up the road, moving slowly.

There are no lights, except for car headlights, and, for long stretches, there's rock wall on the right and drop-offs to the left. I was driving, and, after a few miles, I was disturbed by a light, reflected in the rearview mirror, shining in my face,. It was just one light, and the sideview mirror told me it wasn't coming from a car behind us.

At first I was a little miffed that Barbara, sitting in the backseat, would play a joke on a dangerous road by shining her flashlight into my eyes off the mirror. I said, "Barb, don't shine that flashlight"; and, even as I was saying it, I remembered that I had placed our gear, including the flashlights, into the trunk when we reached the car.

As Barb was denying the accusation, I also noticed that the light, although rather bright, did not affect my vision. I could see the road ahead clearly. I could also see that the light was coming from just behind my rear window, as if someone was sitting on my trunk shining a flashlight into the car.

After the experience out on the lava field, we all just chuckled and accepted the light. Hey, either someone was still escorting us, or, maybe, they were just having a little mischievous fun. No harm done.

Then the light went out. Seconds later, though, the light was shining in through the front passenger window. The light was shining right past Janine's face and onto my right cheek, and it was warm.

This was even more physically impossible than the light through the rear window, because the right side of the car was very close to solid lava walls. There was no clearance for a car, and very little room for even a motorcycle. Besides, it was exceedingly quiet.

That light shone through the window onto my face for over a mile. I had no fear or resistance. Then it stopped. We felt like we were on our own again.

Back driving on Oʻahu one day, I stopped for a red light. An elderly, disheveled, yet noble-looking Polynesian woman with white hair approached my car asking for money.

I instantly "knew" to give her as much as I could, which was ten dollars. Our eyes met, she blessed me, and I blessed her, too.

Was this Madame Pele, and was I repaying her assistance on Kīlauea? Was this one of her helpers? Was this just another Soul, another doorway into the same Cosmic Sea of which Pele is a current? Does it matter?

The White Dog of Mauna Loa

Bernard G. Mendonca

No reminiscence of Mauna Loa Observatory would be complete without mentioning the white dog of Mauna Loa. Much has been told about the mysterious phantom dog that would appear on the mountain to forewarn of a volcanic eruption. Hawaiian legend relates a tale of Pele, who is the fire goddess of the volcanoes on Mauna Loa, and her companion dog, whom she would send as a messenger to alert the people whenever an eruption was imminent.

The white dog was first noticed by the observatory staff during the latter part of 1959. At that time the staff were living on site for up to a week at a time on rotating shifts. Because of this housekeeping, a rubbish dump was soon developed to the west of the observatory. The contention of the staff was that a stray white dog had discovered the dump and foraged it for food. Attempts by the staff to befriend it and later to capture it, no matter how persistent or devious, failed. The dog for some reason would have nothing to do with the observatory staff. Soon the dog disappeared and was presumed to have found its way back to the populated regions of the island. In December 1959, Kīlauea Iki erupted.

To the amazement of the staff the dog reappeared at the observatory several months later and again was spotted intermittently for a month or so and then disappeared. This pattern of appearances and disappearances continued until 1966. Since then, to my knowledge, no one has seen the dog.

Its appearances or disappearances were never regular, and at times it was seen at the summit as well as farther down the access road to the observatory. It would never have anything to do with anyone and whenever pursued would always easily outdistance its pursuers over the rough lava and run to the top of the mountain.

The staff could never determine where it obtained food when it was not at the dump (months at a time) in the desolate environment of the mountain nor why, if it did descend the mountain when it was not seen, it did return to roam the mountaintop for months at a time. This was especially puzzling in view of the fact that the staff sometimes discovered lost hunters' dogs wandering close to the observatory, always in the most pitiful condition. In every case, starvation and exposure to the elements had just about done in these hunters' dogs.

Concerning the belief that the white dog was a messenger of pending eruptions, it is true that it was sighted sometimes before an eruption, but it was also sighted many other times when no eruption occurred.

The dog did create a problem for the staff in that when a staff member would describe the appearance of the dog to visiting scientists or to the public the response would invariably be looks of worry and discomfort or of concern and a fear that this staff member had finally gone stark crazy.

The story of the dog was definitely out of place among scientific endeavors at the observatory, and soon the staff members were hesitant to talk about it to anyone they did not know. To this day the mystery of the white dog is just that—a mystery.

We Meet a Scientist

David Hallsted

"I can't believe that we are getting up this early on our vacation, Susan," I say to my wife. We both struggle to get out of bed at 6 a.m. to see the lava flow down by the sea before the sun gets too bright.

We quickly put on clothes, grab jackets, grab breakfast ingredients, and head out to the rental car in front of our rental cottage in Volcano.

The drive to the lava flow is silent. I am barely awake. We are in a hurry to see the lava before sunrise.

I better keep to the speed limit. I'll probably run into a nēnē *now when I least expect it,* I say to myself as we drive through the park. I start to see the sky lighten. We descend the mountainside down the long winding road to the lava flow.

We finally arrive at the site. Susan directs me to do the u-turn to park going out. I am so glad I married her. Even when we are tired, she still is doing the thinking for both of us.

We silently get out of the car and start walking toward the temporary structures. *It is already light; I hope we can still see the lava,* I think, too tired to speak aloud.

For some unknown reason, as we walk toward the trailhead, I have an impulse to inspect the cars along the way. I notice that out of the seven cars, locals own three.

A faint hint of sulfur wisps through the air as we pick up the pace to the yellow reflectors marking the trail. I notice that a family dressed in traditional Island clothing and flip-flops is leaving the lava. They look like locals to me; that is one car down.

"David, this flow just happened this month," Susan exclaims, as I, too, look at the sign marking the April 2003 lava. I remember that the rangers at the Volcanoes Park station said that there was a new flow, but I did not expect to be walking on it.

We follow the yellow markers over the crumbled broken bit of black, brittle earth. We come upon a street sign engulfed by the flow. A caution marker is inside the pit of a lava tube that has collapsed. I begin to wonder if this trail is safe as our feet crunch along the path. All the while Susan is taking digital photos of our adventure.

We talk with another tourist couple who are leaving the lava flow. They tell us, "You will know when the trail ends; just follow the markers."

I ask Susan, "What do they mean 'we will know'?"

"They probably mean that it will be too hot to go any further," she says.

"Oh, yeah." I remember now that the rangers said

the flow changes all the time. Where the trail was once safe could now be hazardous, they said. I start to be alert at every step I take.

The wind perfumes us with the sulfur scent. We see people standing still. This must be the place to see the lava. We are close, so I pick up the pace. We have been hiking for twenty minutes.

The heat is intense when we arrive. I now understand what the previous tourists said. We stop to look around for something. I am not sure what that should be.

We spot a veteran photographer who is leaving the area. He tells two female tourists about the lava flow into the sea up the trail. He must be a local; who else would know where lava flows into the sea off this trail? That's another local car accounted for.

We both start to notice the red cracks in the black surface of lava, where new, molten lava will possibly come out.

"I did not expect to be able to walk up and touch the flowing lava. This is way too close!" I exclaim with surprise.

No longer do the yellow reflectors speak of caution when the red-hot lava cracks burn of danger.

Three additional tourists stroll past our area and off the yellow marked route. "What are they thinking?" I ask Susan. "This whole area is active." But after watching for lava and seeing none, I think it may be possible to view lava flowing in the area where the tourists went. I am feeling braver and start to walk over there.

"STOP!" I hear, but no word is spoken.

"Susan, I have been told to stop. I think I will do

that. The voice did not say that we are in danger. But to just stop."

We stay where we are. Then I see our first lava flow.

"Susan, look over there, at the red cracks . . . "

"I see it," Susan says, as she begins to take pictures.

We both look as the molten earth lifts up a cap of previously laid lava and new lava bursts out of the tube. A wave of lava continues to flow down from the open tube.

So that is how ropy lave is formed.

I happen to notice a female photographer who is extremely close to the new lava oozing out of the cracks. She is a strawberry blond with hair down to her midback. I would guess that she is in her late twenties to early thirties. She is taking photos with her telephoto lens very close to the lava. She walks about the lava, examining the flow, scrutinizing each layer of molten ooze.

"People like her are dangerous," huffed Susan.

"I don't know; maybe she knows what she's doing."

It seems that she does know what she is doing. There is red-hot lava flowing in tubes all around her, yet she walks about the lava flow not once looking at her footing.

She goes back to her green daypack, puts her camera away, and takes out food to eat. She eats standing, carefully examining the new flow. I notice that a single yellow daisy is sewn on the flap of her daypack.

We continue to watch a fiery crack in the lava

burp the molten rock, slurping down the side. I glance at another red crack and tell Susan to get ready. She says that we will try to get a short movie of this lava flow. She frantically makes changes to the digital camera for the short movie as my eyes are glued to the next flow.

There it goes. The red express flips the top off the cold lava. This is a good one. It oozes for eighteen seconds.

After filming that flow, we watch some lesser flows for a while. Susan notices, as we sit down, that the ground under our bottoms is warm to the touch. There must be lava flowing under all of this new rock! We eventually decide to leave and eat breakfast at the shelter. I happen to notice the female photographer grabbing her daypack to leave also.

As we leave the area, the female photographer starts to talk to us.

"Did you see the lava come out! How the lava flipped the top off and came out! Wasn't that great! You know, you should go over to the water where the lava is flowing into the sea. I mean . . . you know . . . not that you should . . . but if you could. You know what I mean?"

Dumbfounded at having been spoken to, Susan and I do not reply. There is not enough time to reply. As she spoke her words, she has walked from the side of us to in front of us. She finishes talking, turns her back, and is off in a hurry. She is able to walk on this uneven surface very quickly. She speaks and acts with the enthusiasm of a fourteen-year-old girl about to meet the person of her dreams.

Tired and hungry, and feeling a bit sick from the

gaseous fumes, Susan and I start to look again at each step we take back to the car. Susan and I are careful with our footing, as a slip could bring a severe cut from the glass-sharp edges of the new lava rock. A few moments later, I look up to see if I can see the female photographer ahead of us. I look ahead and do not see her. I pause. I look off to each side and cannot see her. I look all around, and the only people I see are the tourists at the lava flow. There is quite a distance to still walk before we hit the pavement. There is no way she could have made it to a car that quickly. There is no place to hide in the bumpy lava flow unless one could just disappear. Then it hits me.

"Susan, that was Pele! I read about her appearing to people and then disappearing the minute they look away."

Susan seemed stunned at the suggestion and said nothing.

All the time we were walking back, I kept a sharp eye out for the female photographer. Even when we had breakfast at the shelter, I inspected each passer-by. Then I remembered the dream of Pele I had when we first came to the island on our honeymoon.

The female photographer had acted exactly as Pele had done ten years ago in my dream. The Pele I dreamt of had an affinity for details. She would sprint down from the mountainside to see exactly where each push of ropy lava stopped. She would study each molten burp of lava to know if that was enough for the desired formation. Her meticulous care for details was matched by her patience for exactness until the process was perfected. She would then sprint back up the mountainside to start the whole process again.

Yes, the Pele I know is a scientist in love with her work, wanting all to enjoy it.

P.S. Later I check to see if we have pictures of Pele. We do, but in each photo, she has her head conveniently looking away from the camera. She does not miss a step.

A *Pilialoha* with Pele

Michael Sturrock

I was fourteen years old the year Kīlauea Iki erupted, and it was, truly, unforgettable. The volcano
began erupting in November 1959 and it continued
erupting quite a while. Through the months that followed the beginning of the eruption, the sky over the
Hawaiian Islands got very red because of all the ash
in the atmosphere.

If I remember correctly, the eruption had a fire
spume two thousand feet high, and the ash that
accumulated in the atmosphere over the Islands created brilliant sunsets.

One evening while I was reading the *Honolulu
Star Bulletin*, I looked at a picture on page one that
showed the extent of the ash cloud over the entire
Hawaiian Islands, and, you know, it looked oddly
familiar.

I just started turning the newspaper around until
there it was—the cloud formation was in the shape

of the Big Island of Hawai'i, where the eruption was occurring.

When I saw this, I commented to my mother that Pele must be putting on this fire show in honor of her old friend Uncle George Lycurgus, who had died at 101 years of age during the eruption.

For most of the second half of his life, Uncle George—that's what everyone called him—had watched over the Volcano House at Kīlauea and had developed a *pilialoha*, or close companionship, with Pele.

To this day, as I look back on this event, I feel it was Pele's way of saying aloha to her old friend.

Pele's Birth Announcement

Dwynn Kamai

Agnes Kamai Yuen, "Moloka'i Grandma" as we affectionately knew her, was a tiny but very strong woman. Grandma was a jack of all trades and master of most. She worked at the state hospital and was an educator, award-winning artist, mother of eight, and grandmother of many.

At the time of this tale, the family had been living in Waiākea on the Big Island. You see, Grandpa Kamai was a heavy equipment operator, and many times had to uproot the family to go where the company sent him. Grandma had already raised three children and was *hāpai* with the fourth.

One day, as Grandma was walking down the trail on one of her frequent visits to the volcanoes, she was approached by a mysterious older woman dressed in white. She had long salt-and-pepper hair, and with her was a white dog. As the two met, the woman stopped Grandma and told her that she would deliver a boy and on that same day the volcano would erupt.

On July 1, 1931, Moloka‘i Grandma delivered my father, Heine Kamai (her only son) and yes, that volcano erupted. We have always teased Dad that Hawai‘i celebrated his birth with the natural fireworks of the volcano.

Madame Pele, as we believe the woman in the story to have been, visits as a young, beautiful woman as well as an older, mysterious woman. My family has encountered her in both versions.

Moloka‘i Grandma and Dad are gone now, but their legacies live on.

ON OTHER ISLANDS

Madame Pele Visited Waikīkī

David Soares

Years ago, when I worked for the Hilton Hawaiian Village for six weeks in housekeeping, the maids were afraid to walk down the hallways. This was in 1958, when they made the movie *South Pacific*, and I met Mitzi Gaynor and Rosanno Brazzi.

On certain nights, the maids used to see Pele down in the hallways wearing a red *mu'umu'u*. They all were afraid to walk down the hallways at a certain hour. I was the only one who dared to walk down the hallways.

Mitzi Gaynor and Rosanno Brazzi had a big party to celebrate the end of shooting of *South Pacific* on Kaua'i. So the head housekeeper set up for the party in the hallway. When I walked in at that hour the Hawaiians and Filipinos were going around the hallways and up the stairways to avoid running into Pele.

I never did encounter Madame Pele, never had what you'd call an introduction, but Pele seemed to be very much alive and real to those who saw her. She used to appear regularly at the Hilton Hawaiian Village, but some said it was just the ghost of a woman who died there. I don't know. That was an old burial ground, back in the 1700s. This is the word handed down by generations.

I'll be sixty-six this year, and almost fully alert, and a real *kolohe*, Hawaiian rascal, but I never did see Madame Pele there, but I saw the fear on the faces of the people who did.

Me? I was never afraid. When I was a little boy my father told me, "Only fear a living soul. The dead ones can't hurt you." Isn't that true?

Ride to the Source

Rick Carroll

Our horse's forelocks are wrapped in cowhide to guard against the razor's edge of lava. Slowly, we pick our way around jagged shards of *'a'ā*. If we spill in this *terra terrabilis* we surely will be slashed to shreds.

I lean far forward in my saddle as we head from Mākena up the south side of Haleakalā on Maui's 'Ulupalakua Ranch, a vertical spread on a nearly two-mile-high volcano that's not done yet.

This old volcano is officially classified as dormant, which means it can go off at any moment. Not today, we hope.

We are riding to the source, to Pu'u Māhoe, the last lava flow from Haleakalā crater that went off about 1780, the last time Maui experienced a volcanic eruption.

In the deep time of geology that's only yesterday. Perouse, the first white man to set foot on Maui, on May 29, 1786, described "a shore made hideous by an ancient lava flow," and sailed on, never to be seen again, yet another mystery of the Pacific.

The lava reflects the sun's heat deep into my bones. I am glad to have an old *lauhala* hat on my head and water in my saddlebag.

No one knows exactly when Haleakalā last erupted, but everyone knows it is long overdue. I wonder when it will roar again.

The thought of eruption is very much on my mind as we ride to the last crater that erupted on Maui.

We ride by *kiawe* with stiletto thorns that can pierce a leather boot, past old, sun-bleached bones (whose? I wonder), across wide stretches of nothing but lava that once was alive and dribbling down to the shore.

Nothing stirs in this dead zone except fine clouds of suffocating red dust kicked up by our horses. I pull a red bandanna across my face as we ride on deeper into Pele land.

We rein in at the source: a classic cone crater with a tell-tale tongue of *pāhoehoe* sticking out its downhill lip.

I walk to the edge and look down the throat of this old crater's hell-hole and see only dead ashes. Way down there somewhere, I know, the pot still boils.

From the crater to the sea, Maui looks like an eighteenth-century engraving of itself, an island frozen in time, smothered by miles of lava in every direction as far as the eye can see, a black silent place, Pele's world.

Out of the sun-struck sea a whale leaps, my horse flicks its tail, and in that very moment, as I stand there on the dormant crater, Maui seems to exist only in the primeval. I am glad to head on down the narrow trail and return to the present.

HITCHHIKING

A Rainy Night on Old Pali Highway

Russell L. Stevens

My wife and I lived in Hawai'i from 1938 until 1942, when I entered the U.S. Navy for the war's duration. We lived a most interesting life in various places throughout the Pacific, but of all the ones in which we lived, Hawai'i held the most interest for us. One incident we experienced there stands alone as inexplicable and enchanting.

On an occasion in 1938, we were driving in a station wagon high up on the Old Pali Road in Nu'uanu Valley, barely able to see through a very heavy downpour of rain. A couple of miles before the road reached the Pali, we saw an old lady sloshing along the puddled path on the side of the road, barefoot and wearing an old, *mu'umu'u*-style, white, and not very clean dress.

I stopped the car alongside the curb, rolled down the window, and asked if she needed a ride. The woman was rather tall, quite slender, not very attractive, and obviously of Hawaiian ancestry. Apparently she spoke no English, and instinctively I opened the rear door and tried to get her into the car to converse with her. The only thing she said over and over, with undeniable insistence, was "Kalihi uka." (Kalihi is an area, and *uka* means "the back of.")

After several minutes of indecision and attempts to learn the nature of the problem, my wife and I decided to turn around and go back toward 'Ewa, to Kalihi Valley. Near Kalihi, while driving on King Street, we spotted a Hawaiian lady we knew well, who lived near our home. We stopped and asked if she would talk with our passenger and ascertain what she wanted. She agreed, and talked with the lady for several minutes.

Finally, with a shrug, she said that, although she spoke the Hawaiian language well, she could not understand much of what the old woman was saying. She said the woman's grammar and vocabulary seemed very old and obsolete. She made one more attempt, finally gave up, and apologized for not being of much assistance.

We left our friend and started again, this time going *mauka* up Kalihi Street with the old woman frequently and firmly saying "Kalihi *uka*" to us and motioning with her hands for us to take her ever deeper into Kalihi Valley. The further we went, the heavier it rained, and eventually we came to a large stream that was flowing full and fast, precluding any further reliance upon the car.

With the old woman continuing her "Kalihi *uka*" directions and her hand and arm motions, I got out of the car, motioned for her to get out also, and led her to the edge of the stream. After showing her by gesture that I could not take her further, I motioned that she should get on my back, piggyback style.

I turned my back toward her, backed up, and extended my arms for her assistance. She got on my back, and I was completely surprised to find that I felt hardly any weight. She felt as light as a proverbial feather. I waded across the stream, barely keeping her from getting soaked by the flow, and deposited her on the far edge of the water. She broke into a huge smile and waved as I started back to the car.

I arrived back on the other side thoroughly soaked, got into the car, talked briefly with my wife, and started the engine. Both of us turned to wave a final good-bye, but the old lady was not there. She had completely disappeared and there was no place where she could have vanished.

We scanned the entire area within eyesight and saw nothing but rain, weeds, bushes, and a closed water-reserve area fence and gate a few feet from the streambed. We returned home, and since that time have talked about the incident times without number. The old lady's vanishing act was perfect in execution.

Over the next few days, I made every attempt I could think of to ascertain the identity of the woman with whom we had shared a true mystery. I checked the police, newspapers, governmental institutions, and other sources to find out if there were any missing persons reports. All attempts were to no avail. I went door-to-door to talk with people who lived closest to the disappearance, without finding out who the old woman was.

Finally, we told our story to Clara Mokumaia, a close Hawaiian friend who was a retired principal of Moanalua School on the Damon Estate grounds. After we finished our story, she rose to her feet, became very animated, did a quick hula step and said, "My children, you are exceedingly fortunate. You met, and helped, Pele. All will go well with you in Hawai'i."

The details of our encounter, with whom we can only speculate, are as vivid today as they were in that long ago rainstorm. And our love of Hawai'i has never faded.

The Passenger

Rick Carroll

She stood in shimmering heat waves along Queen Kaʻahumanu Highway on a hot October day. I couldn't believe anybody would be standing in the sun at high noon on what seemed like the hottest day of the year. I thought at first the woman in the white dress might be a mirage. Dark skin, the color of coffee, Caribbean maybe; black hair in dreadlocks, she looked real as a rainbow. She stuck out her thumb and I stopped.

My day full of strange encounters began in Honolulu at the airport. A security guard wanted to inspect my carry-on.

"Oh, I love your books," she said, finding only spooky books in my bag. I gave her one. She gave me a *mahalo,* and waved me through.

On line at Starbucks a Charles Manson look-a-like, one of the terminal's homeless denizens, hit me up for three dollars. He wanted "a wet, double tall, French vanilla latte." His outrageous request made me laugh. I gave him a buck.

While waiting for my coffee I was paged repeatedly: " . . . please return to the security gate." I finally got my coffee and went back to find I'd dropped my ticket to Kona during the security check.

I ran to the gate only to find my plane was late. By the time I got to the Big Island the Budget rental car outfit was out of cars.

"We have a ten-passenger van you can have for the same price as an economy sedan."

"It's just me," I said.

"It's all we have," the clerk said. She handed me the keys to what looked like a Roberts Overnighter tour bus.

That's how I came to be all alone driving an air-conditioned van big enough for ten people on Queen Ka'ahumanu Highway on the Big Island of Hawai'i on a hot October day.

My destination was Waimea School, where I'd been invited to read from my books as part of the Marriott Outrigger Waikoloa's annual spooky "talk story" event.

I saw the hitchhiker just after leaving the airport. With an empty ten-passenger van, I decided to give her a lift.

I stopped, she got in, and I immediately felt

something was wrong but didn't know what. The chilled van seemed warmer with her aboard.

"Where're you going?"

"Waimea," she said.

"Me too," I said.

"Do you live there?"

"No," she said, "just visiting."

She was neither young nor old, but somewhere in between, with caramel skin, charcoal hair, bright, clear eyes and a soft voice that sounded like music.

She carried neither suitcase nor backpack, only a white canvas bag stuffed with newspapers and magazines, and handwritten notes on yellow legal pads.

She had a musty aroma of sweat and something flammable. I thought the rental van had a gas leak.

Queen Kaʻahumanu Highway is unique in Hawaiʻi. The two-lane black asphalt not only runs through twenty miles of black lava landscape, but also crosses over several layers of historic lava flows and under four of the island's five volcanoes—Kohala, Huālalai, Mauna Loa, and Mauna Kea. Pele land if there ever was.

Most passersby see only a bleak charcoal expanse, but my passenger knew and identified each and every lava flow with evident pride as if each flow were an object of art in her private collection.

"Kaʻūpūlehu flowed to the sea in 1801," she said as we passed under Huālalai Volcano. "It filled Kīholo Bay . . . "

"... and the 1859 Mauna Loa flow ran from nine thousand feet near the summit to the sea ... "

"... the Kanikū flow covered Waikoloa and ran into the fishponds at 'Anaeho'omalu ... "

Although I had no way to verify the truth of her words, her keen recitation startled me.

"How do you know all this?" I asked.

"Just do," she said. "It's my hobby."

We rode in silence for a mile or so. I half expected her to ask for a cigarette—a common request from Pele, the fire goddess.

"Don't you want to ask me for a cigarette?'

"I don't smoke," she said, smiling.

We rode on in silence.

"Are you sure you're not Madame Pele?" I finally asked. I couldn't help it.

"Oh no," she said. "I'm not Madame Pele."

"How do I know?"

"Believe me," she laughed.

"I'm not sure I do," I said.

In misty rain, we approached Waimea town. She said good-bye and thanks at the T-intersection.

"I'll get out here," she said at the stoplight. She opened the door and jumped out. She cut across the corner gas station; I half expected the gas pumps to burst into flames.

That never happened. Something just as startling did. As I watched her walk away, she disappeared. Vanished into thin air. One minute she was there, the next she was gone, like that. I asked the gas station attendant if he'd seen the woman in white.

"No, brah, see nothing."

I found Waimea School library full of kids waiting to hear spooky tales that Friday afternoon. The library was cool and quiet, I was hot and sweaty.

"Are you okay?" one of the librarians asked. "You look like you've seen a ghost."

"I'm not really sure, but I think I just gave a ride to a woman who may have been Madame Pele."

The librarian had a sympathetic smile. "I know," she said. "It happens a lot here."

That night at a dinner party hosted by Patti Cook, who knows everybody in Waimea, I told my story to the other guests and asked if they had ever seen the woman hitchhiking along the Queen's highway or walking in their town.

Now, Waimea's a very small town, and surely someone would have seen a woman in a white dress with dreadlocks who knew a lot about old volcanoes, but nobody ever had, at least that's what they told me.

The Night
Pele Visited Hanauma Bay

Dominic Kealoha Aki

The night this happened, I was a junior at Castle High in Kāneʻohe, and my friends and I were going camping at Hanauma Bay. At that time you could camp down there, and many school groups and families used to camp there a lot.

We got a late start, and it was about 10:30 when my friends picked me up. We were just passing Sandy Beach out toward Hālona Cove, where the blowhole is, and on the *mauka* side of the highway where you enter the winding sea cliff road by the bus stop is where we saw her.

And she was in her old woman's form.

Apparently when she travels around the Islands, she appears in different forms—as a young woman dressed in red, or as an old woman dressed in white. Sometimes she appears as a fireball, a young child, or a small dog.

But this was an old woman.

She was about five feet one or five feet two,

maybe one hundred pounds, and she had long silver hair down to her waist. She was wearing a white *pāʻū,* the skirt, and *kīhei,* the shoulder cover, both of tapa. She looked like she was in a toga outfit. She was walking with the aid of a cane.

As we passed her, she turned to look at us the same time I turned to look at her. I still remember her face to this day.

That's an isolated road. No one travels that road at night except maybe a few fishermen or passing motorists. There's no one out walking around this deserted area of the island, not at that hour—about 11:30.

As we passed her I told my friend Steven to pick her up, but he declined.

He said, "I'm not stopping for anybody."

So I reminded him that if we didn't stop, it would be bad luck, and he said, "Well, that's not Pele."

"Of course, it's Pele," I said. Who else would it be?"

So while we were arguing this, we passed the turnout at Hālona Point.

And so he said, "Well, we've already passed the turnout. Besides, I don't believe those Pele stories, anyway."

As soon as he said that a big white bird flew in through the sunroof of his car—an old Capri. Sunroofs were real popular right about that time, real trendy.

Anyway, this big white bird flew in through the sunroof and started banging about in the car and we almost crashed—almost lost control and piled up. Steve pulled over and chased the bird out and we just stared at each other in amazement and were going, "What was that?"

"Eh, I told you. I told you. I told you. If you don't pick her up it's gonna be bad luck. You almost killed both of us."

He said, "That's coincidence."

"Coincidence? First off, you've seen the lady. We both agreed she looks like Pele, right?"

"Right."

"Right after you said you don't believe in Pele and you're not going to pick her up, did this big white bird fly in the sunroof?"

"Yes."

"Well, birds normally don't fly at night, do they?"

"No."

"I never saw a bird fly INTO a car at night, much less come in through the sunroof. We don't even know what kind of bird that was."

He said, "Oh, I think it's a seagull."

I reminded him we don't have seagulls in Hawai'i.

So he was going, "Well, it's just coincidence."

Anyway, we got down to the bay and told this story to our friends there, and they didn't believe us either. They went, "What? Are you guys crazy? What are you on? You guys drinking already?"

"Steve, tell them did you see an old Hawaiian woman walking along the road?"

"Yes."

"Did a big white bird fly in through the sunroof?"

"Well yes, that's true, too, but it's coincidence."

While we were arguing this point, one of the

guys saw a golden light appear on the left side of the cliffs. (If you're down at the bay looking out, you see sea cliffs on both sides of the bay, with the bay in the center.) When we looked, the rest of us saw it too.

"What's that? What's that?" one guy asked.

"It's probably some fishermen," somebody else replied.

Then we all observed the golden light descend the left side of the cliff, move across the bay, ascend the right side of the cliff, and disappear into the night.

Around the campfire it got pretty quiet. Everyone was kinda spooked out.

"What was that?" somebody asked again.

"I think," I said, "that it was probably Madam Pele in her fireball form just letting us know, you know, that she's passing by this area to remind us to pick her up next time."

Nobody said a word. We were too spooked.

Because had that golden light stayed on the left side of the cliff—well, that could be fishermen up there. Or if it had gone down on the water, it could have been fisherman out on a boat. But when the fireball went across the bay and ascended the very steep right side of the cliff almost alongside the angle of the cliff—that was undeniable.

I wouldn't be surprised if we were the only ones who saw the fireball that night.

That's my true-life Pele story; it happened twenty years ago, but I'll never forget it.

A Red Jacket for Honey-Girl

Michael Sunnafrank

Eric and Pudge, two students from a previous class I took to Hawai'i, had decided to meet up with me and the current class to visit friends in Pāhala on the Big Island. Eric picked up Vanessa in O'ahu, and they were off to the Honolulu Airport. That is where things started to go wrong.

Their luggage was loaded on the plane to Hilo, but they were bumped. There were no more flights to Hilo that day that could accommodate all of them, so they decided to fly to the Kona-side airport. Eric works for Enterprise Rent-A-Car in Minnesota, so when they landed they decided to head to Enterprise. Enterprise is located off-airport in Kailua-Kona, so they called to get a ride. By the time they got there the last vehicle had just been rented. They got a ride back to the airport to rent from a different company, at full price of course.

Now they were off to Hilo to get their luggage. As they exited the airport they saw a man and a girl hitchhiking and stopped for them. As it turns out, they were going to Hilo also.

Off they went for the Saddle Road. Vanessa started up a conversation with the pair and discovered the man had hitchhiked to Kailua that day to pick up his daughter for the weekend. Now they were on their way back to his home in Hilo.

The girl, a young teen or close, was very pretty. She was excited about the jacket she was wearing. It was red and the in-brand with teens that year. She had just received it as a Christmas present. She talked a lot about how much she liked that jacket.

As they neared Hilo, Eric asked where they would like to be dropped. The man said their final destination was up on Kīlauea. Eric told him they were headed for Pāhala and would be going over the volcano as soon as they picked up their luggage.

The man said they needn't bother and to let them off by a phone booth. They would just call friends who would be headed their way. Eric pulled over at a gas station that had a phone, dropped them off, and they all said aloha. When they left the station, the man and girl were nearing the phone booth.

When they were about half a block from the gas station, Vanessa noticed the girl had left the red jacket in the car. They made a quick U-turn to return the jacket, but when they got to the station the man and girl were nowhere to be seen.

The three of them couldn't have been gone from the station more than thirty seconds, hardly enough time to drop coins in the pay phone, dial, and get an answer. Certainly not enough time to get picked up. Vanessa checked in the station, but they weren't there and no one had seen them. Eric drove around looking for them for about ten minutes, but there was no trace.

Eric, Pudge, and Vanessa all hated giving up the search, but it was obvious they weren't going to find the pair. They picked up their luggage and headed for Pāhala. When I saw them there they told me the whole story. I suggested they might want to give the jacket to the daughter of one of our local friends. Vanessa got the jacket and they gave it to Honey-Girl.

Now it was Honey's turn to be very excited, as it not only fit her perfectly but was just the jacket she had been wanting and red was her favorite color.

We have talked about the events of that day several times. So many missteps in one short day: the luggage sent to Hilo, no more room on the several remaining flights to Hilo (isn't there generally room on those Hilo flights?), off to Kailua-Kona, no cars at the off-airport Enterprise, back to the airport to rent a car, the man and girl waiting for a ride to Hilo just outside the rental car area, the pretty girl so excited about her in-brand red jacket but leaving it behind, and the disappearing pair who first said they had to get to Hilo but when they got to Hilo indicated they were headed for Kīlauea.

One of the locals in Pāhala suggested this could be a Pele sighting. The girl was pretty, the jacket was red, the pair were headed over the Saddle Road to Kīlauea, and they pretty conclusively vanished.

I have heard stories of Pele hitchhiking but don't recall any with her pairing up with a man to do so. I have heard of her appearing as a pretty young woman in red but not as a young teen. But I suppose Pele can do as she wishes. One thing is certain. Honey-Girl was destined to get the red jacket she so wanted.

The Hitchhiker of Laupāhoehoe

Cheryl Zimbra

On a crisp and clear morning, shortly past the midnight hour, a young man in his twenties travels alone along the dark stretch of the road leading to Hilo town on the Big Island of Hawai'i. As he passes Laupāhoehoe he sees a figure in the distance that appears to be hitchhiking along the side of the deserted highway.

Upon nearing the figure he realizes that it is a woman dressed entirely in black. She wears a long hooded coat and long black gloves. Feeling she is in distress, he pulls over and offers her a ride. She graciously accepts.

The dark of the early morning sky doesn't enable the young man to get a close look at her, but trusting that she is harmless, he continues along. After having traveled awhile in complete silence, the driver tries in vain to make conversation with his passenger.

Deciding she has probably fallen asleep, curiosity overwhelms him and he wants to catch a glimpse of the quiet stranger. Not wanting to take his eyes off the road for too long, he cautiously leans forward and is unprepared for what he finds: nothing but darkness peering out from behind her hooded cloak.

Beginning to worry and unsure of what is taking place, he glances down at the rest of her and realizes she doesn't have any feet.

Panic-stricken, he yanks the vehicle over and rushes off to find a pay phone. Upon returning to the car, he finds she has disappeared.

Feeling vulnerable and frightened, he decides it would be better to drive the rest of the way home than to stay in the middle of nowhere, alone, until the morning comes. In shock, he gets back into his car and forces himself to continue. Inside the car he finds himself shivering and rolls up the windows to keep warm. Funny, he thinks to himself, that he hadn't noticed how cold it was outside. But the inside of the car continues to get colder even with the windows rolled up.

Unable to keep his mind off of the ghostly passenger, he glances down to where she once sat. In her place remains an indentation, as if someone is still sitting next to him.

The Girl by the Side of the Road

Rick Carroll

I am telling this story because after she told it to me she disappeared. I don't know what happened to her. All I know is what she told me.

We met on Maui at Borders one night when I told spooky tales from my books. At the end of the evening I asked if anyone in the audience had a story to share.

Hands rose slowly. A woman told about the "pressing" spirit that held her down in a Kula bed and breakfast, a young boy had seen a fireball in the old Japanese graveyard at Ka'uiki Head in Hāna.

A bookstore clerk, Lynne, I think her name was, said she had a Pele story, but she didn't want to tell it in front of others; people might think she was, you know, *lōlō*. After everyone left that night, I listened to her story. This is what she told me:

"One night driving from 'Īao Valley I saw this young woman hitchhiking. We've all heard the stories about Madame Pele hitchhiking, but I always thought she hitchhiked somewhere else, on the Big Island, I guess.

"I never heard of Madame Pele hitchhiking on Maui, not in Kahului. Every story I ever heard, she was never a young woman. She's supposed to be an old woman. This was a young woman.

"Young women hitchhike on Maui, but not usually at night, not in Kahului.

"*Something's wrong,* I thought, *something doesn't feel right.* I decided not to stop and pick her up. I drove by, and as I did I glanced at her, and she looked right at me, and smiled.

"I drove on, and when I got to the next light I couldn't believe my eyes. There she was again, standing by the side of the road, thumb out, a smile on her face.

"I had to look, to make sure it was her, and not another young woman hitchhiking. It was her.

"I didn't know what to do: Stop, go, look, smile, wave, what?

"The light turned green, and I drove by her. I tried not to look, but I had to; at the last minute I stole a glance. She looked straight at me and smiled again, a big, eerie smile.

"I was spooked. I kept driving and started wondering if I was seeing things when just ahead at the next stoplight I could see her again, standing by the side of the road, thumb out, hitchhiking, smiling at me.

"I panicked. I just stepped on it and drove as fast as I could past her, down the road to Borders, jumped out, locked my car, and ran inside. I told everyone what happened.

"They said there were only two, maybe three explanations: I'd been seeing things. I'd somehow picked up a wandering spirit. Or Madame Pele was messing with my mind."

That's her story, and I believe her. She got spooked just recalling her encounter. You can't fake real fright.

When I called her a few weeks later to ask a follow-up question, her phone number was disconnected, and there was no new number. The store manager at Borders told me the clerk up and quit her job one day and nobody saw her again. Everyone remembered her story, though.

I don't know what happened to her, but I'd like to know if she's okay.

And if some night between ʻĪao Valley and Kahului you see the girl by the side of the road, I'd sure like to hear from you.

Pele Goes Shopping in Kāne'ohe

Fox Harmon

Since my move to Hawai'i a few years ago I've heard plenty of accounts of Pele encounters but I never expected to have one of my own. My own background is steeped in a cultural sense of the spiritual, so when it happened on the windward side of O'ahu I reacted not with fright but surprise and respect.

It was approximately 9:30 p.m., one Wednesday night in April 2001. I was dropping a friend off from work. After leaving him at his house I pulled up to the stop sign at Mikiola Drive and Kāne'ohe Bay Drive. I checked for traffic both ways, and seeing none I checked to my right again. I was startled to see an old woman with long gray hair standing on the corner under the plumeria tree. She was dressed in a long white *mu'umu'u*.

I knew she wasn't there last I looked, so when she approached my car I already had the thought of

Pele in my head. She tapped on my window, and I rolled it down and asked if I could help her.

She asked me to give her a ride to Kāneʻohe Bay Market. I didn't hesitate, even though I knew the market wasn't even half a block away.

When she got in the car she didn't say much, but I was hit with the smell of pungent earth. I wasn't scared, just a little in awe, and wondering if this was really Pele.

She instructed me to drive around from the back side so I could pull right up in front of the doors to let her out. When she got out of the car and closed the door, I turned to watch her go in. She simply vanished. I knew she couldn't have walked in that quickly.

I couldn't restrain myself from going inside to look for her. The clerk looked at me as if I was a little off—nobody else was in the market—so I didn't bother to explain.

Every time I pass there I always look for that woman in white, just in case she needs a ride.

PELE'S ROCKS

A Lady's Advice

Kalina Chang

My cousin and her husband were attending a seminar on the Big Island, so my husband and I went over to join them for a couple of days. Having some free time, we went up to the North Kohala area. I had been to many places on the Big Island, but had never been to that part before.

We parked on a *pali*, and down below was a black sand beach. There was a trail, and my cousin and her husband wanted to hike down to the beach, so off they went. Not knowing we might do this, I was wearing slippers. My husband didn't feel like hiking, so he was sitting in the car, relaxing.

I wondered if the trail was easy enough to try, wearing slippers. I turned around and there she was: a lady sitting on the rock wall. Her hair was long and white-gray, but her face was young. She smiled and said hello. I told her I was thinking of going down the trail to join my cousin, but didn't know if I could do that with what I was wearing on my feet. Or could I go barefoot?

She said she knew the trail well, and I definitely should go, and wear the slippers because there were some rocks. After I walked to the trailhead, a few feet away, I decided to thank her for the advice. But when I turned around, she was gone. I went on down the trail; in some places it was rocky, but nothing serious.

Later, I asked my husband if he saw the woman. He said he saw her sitting on the rock wall. I asked if he saw her arrive, and he said, "No." Then I asked if he saw her leave, and he said, "No."

That day my cousin decided to take some black sand home with her to California, as she likes to collect small amounts of sand from everywhere. She also took a few rocks from down on the Kohala Coast, though she knew she wasn't supposed to.

Two weeks later she called me. She had boxed up the rocks and was sending them to me to take back to Kohala. Their dog had become extremely sick, and her husband also had some health problems.

I thought about the lady on the wall with her long white hair. Did she encourage me to join them hoping I would be able to persuade them not to take anything? I guess I will always wonder about her.

Next Time Listen to Uncle

Michael Sunnafrank

It was my first time at Ka Lae, the southernmost point in the United States and the likely first landing point of humans on Hawai'i. We could all sense the power of this sacred place. We looked in silence at the lava statue of a chained Hawaiian that Palikapu and friends placed there. Words could not express the sadness we felt at the message it conveyed.

Awed whispers turned to excited chatter as we all walked down to the point. From there Uncle Cliff showed the students the way to the unspeakably beautiful Green Sand Beach.

The green sand had been produced by a volcanic eruption of olivine in the distant past. The sand and the cliffs surrounding the beach are primarily composed of this semiprecious green olivine.

Fortunately, the surf was perfect that day and we all hurried to cool off after the long, hot, dry walk across the lava fields. After a few hours it was time to start back.

Uncle Cliff told my students that no one should take sand from the beach and warned us of the consequences of doing so.

He told us Madame Pele would not want the relatively rare sacred sand to leave this place. But there is always at least one in every crowd who doesn't believe, doesn't listen.

In this crowd it was Snickers. She just had to take some of that green sand with her back to Minnesota. Out of sight of the rest of us, she hid some in her pack.

That evening we all hiked out to the edge to see the lava flow. Again it was time to be awed by the beauty and power of this place. On the way back, Snickers suffered her first consequence.

Walking on a flat stretch of lava she suddenly fell, scraping her leg badly. Once we were sure she was going to be okay we moved on. A few of us began to tease her about taking lava rock or green sand but she denied it.

As we continued back to the cars, some of the students told Cliff and me that Snickers had confessed to taking the green sand.

Cliff told Snickers several stories about bad fortune coming to people who had taken the sand from Pele, but Snickers refused to believe there was any connection between her fall and the green sand.

The next day we were off to O'ahu. Snickers' bad luck continued, and everyone began telling her to let Uncle Cliff take the green sand back to the Big Island when he returned. Even after a car came within a few inches of hitting her, Snickers wasn't budging. That is, not until the incident at Waimea Valley.

We had a whole day planned around the trip to

Waimea. The day was beautiful, as all our days seemed to be. After all, when you are used to minus-twenty-degree temperatures, any day in Hawai'i is bound to be wonderful.

Still, I was careful to make sure I wasn't riding in a car with Snickers. No use taking chances.

At Waimea Valley we learned about precontact life, played traditional Hawaiian games, and swam under the waterfall. The group discovered there were free all-terrain vehicles to try. Just a simple, short oval route. We watched young children taking their turns, and then a few of us decided to try.

Finally, it was Snickers' turn. She got about halfway around that oval when suddenly the accelerator got stuck on full throttle. The brakes wouldn't work, and she careened off the track and down a small cliff.

The ATV rolled over and landed on top of Snickers' leg. My son, Ryan, ran down the hill and lifted the ATV off her. Fortunately, Snickers wasn't hurt too badly. Nothing broken. Nothing a few stitches wouldn't mend.

I talked to the attendants about the incident and learned nothing like this had ever happened before. They were pretty shook up about the whole thing. The next time I visited the valley there were no free ATV rides being offered. I guess a little of Snickers' bad fortune rubbed off on all of us would-be ATVers.

Nothing disastrous had befallen Snickers, but the close calls and minor scrapes had served as effective warnings. Needless to say, Snickers asked Uncle Cliff to return the green sand to where Madame Pele originally placed it.

No Sleep in Pele's World

Michael Dalke

We all know never never take any volcanic rocks. We all know the wrath of Madame Pele. These are things we know. Well, I was involved in an incident that became kind of a nightmare, all because a guy with me actually did that, took rocks from Madame Pele's world.

It happened four or five years ago. We were in Hilo, negotiating a timber deal, and two people with me weren't from Hawai'i. They heard about the volcano. It was going off at the moment, so that evening we said let's drive down and take a look.

We drove to Volcano, had a few drinks at the Volcano House, and then headed down Chain of Craters Road, watching the glow all the way. It was very bright and beautiful, and we were excited to walk in and see the volcano. We came around a corner and—bammmmm! It sounded like we ran over a huge boulder.

What the hell was that? We all got out of the car,

looked around the car, looked under the car, no flat tire, no boulders, no evident problem, the suspension was intact, all four tires good. We saw nothing. We all got back in the car and kept going.

Thirty minutes later, by the time we got down to the end of Chain of Craters Road where the lava runs across the road, plenty of people had already walked in, so we had to turn around at the end of the road and come back to find a parking spot.

We parked, got out, and headed down the road toward the new lava flow. That's when we noticed a pool of oil at the place where you turn around, and we thought, oh, some poor guy is losing oil.

We walked about an hour, got closer to the lava flow, didn't get all the way to see it. It's tough going in the dark across the *pāhoehoe* with only a flash-light, light bobbing, ground uneven, real dark. And we got tired, didn't get close enough to see the lava boiling into the ocean, so we turned around and came back to the car. It was about two in the morning.

Again, we saw the oil pool, and we started laughing at the poor guy who lost his oil, and as we walked toward our car we noticed the oil slick kept going and it went right under our rental car.

Oh, no, we must have hit something up on the road.

One fellow who was with us has car dealerships and knew what to look at under the hood and under the chassis and he found a big hole in the pan. Not one drop of oil left. We pretty well knew if we drove up the hill we'd blow up the rental car. It wouldn't be a good thing.

We decided to just crash there for the night. No

one was going anywhere. We couldn't see anybody. It was pitch dark, no stars, just the eerie red glow of the volcano.

About an hour later, a family came back from the lava, and they were going back up, offered a ride. I said, you guys stay here, I'll go back with them and call a tow truck. Nothing to it. They gave me a ride to Volcano House. That was about three o'clock.

I called Hilo, a tow truck came out, I gave him directions, he went down and got the car, got the other two guys, came back to pick me up at Volcano House. So we're all together again, start climbing into the cab of the tow truck and the driver says, "Not! Cannot! Can only have three in the front seat."

So I had to rent a room for one of the guys, put him up at Volcano House, and the three of us drove back to Hilo, the driver dropped the rental car, dropped us at the Naniloa.

We got two hours sleep. Up again. Called the rental company. Got another car. I raced up to Volcano House to pick up the other guy to drive him back to the next meeting in Hilo.

We got back to Volcano House. Harry was deathly ill in the hotel. He was like white, couldn't go to the meeting. He lay in bed all day. We had the meeting, came back, he was still real sick, so sick he couldn't travel. I noticed three lava rocks sitting on the bed and I said, "Harry, what the hell is that?"

He had done the absolute tabu and picked up rocks in the lava field, and Madame Pele was doing her number on him.

We got him together and caught a five o'clock

plane back to Oʻahu and put him to bed. Next morning he went to the doctor. We mailed the rocks back to the postmaster in Volcano. And three or four days later he was feeling a little bit better but still pretty junk.

He did finally recover. We never did get to see the lava. We never closed the timber deal. All of it, I guess, was not meant to be. I'll never again take anyone to see the volcano who isn't from Hawaiʻi.

Aliens Discovered in Pele's Pit

Rick Carroll

The crewcut man with aquamarine eyes and crafty smile said he'd made one thousand deep-sea dives in the Pacific. He couldn't talk about one hundred. "All in Hawai'i," he said. "Top secret."

On his way home from the far Pacific, this solo traveler passing through Honolulu was lonesome and eager to chat.

We met at Bestsellers at the airport, where I was signing spooky books one afternoon.

"Good stuff," he said, thumbing pages.

"True spooky stories," I replied.

He had some true spooky stories of his own "out there," he said, but couldn't talk about them. When I raised my eyebrows in doubt, he dropped words like "mixed gas diving" and "closed circuit rebreathers," as if to prove he was the real deal.

I pegged him for a spook in a wet suit. He certainly talked the talk, and I listened, a captive of my curiosity, intrigued always by the vocabulary of odd occupations.

While I sold him a book, he said he was on his way back from Bikini.

"Bikini," I said. "Isn't that where America dropped the biggest bomb in world history?"

"Roger, that," he said.

The effects, I knew, were devastating: The fifteen-megaton hydrogen bomb vaporized three islands. Blew a hole in the earth deep into the heart of matter.

Nuclear fallout rained down on fifty thousand square miles of the Pacific Ocean and the Marshall Islands. Bikini, the mother of all Ground Zeroes, one of Earth's most contaminated places, *kapu* since 1954.

I once read that reef sharks won't eat barracudas because they are full of radioactive toxins. That if you ate Bikini coconuts for a year, you might start to glow.

"What do you see down there?" I asked.

"Strange things," he said.

"Really?" I asked, "like what?"

"New forms of life."

"Aliens?"

"You could call them that."

"What do you see in Hawai'i?" I ventured. Never hurts to ask.

"Strange critters," he said. He looked around as if he'd just spilled a top secret overheard by the secret police.

"Gotta go," he said, and vanished in the terminal.

I never saw the crewcut man with aquamarine eyes again, never gave him a thought actually, until the other day while reading the *Star-Bulletin*.

"The new crater on Lōʻihi presents more surprises about the undersea volcano," the Page One headline said.

"Pisces V, Hawaii Undersea Research Laboratory's submersible, returns from an exploration of Pele's Pit."

The Honolulu daily reported on the ongoing deep-sea exploration of Lōʻihi, the new volcano rising to the surface off the Big Island of Hawaiʻi.

Scientists named the peak of the submarine volcano Pele's Dome, in honor of the Hawaiian fire goddess, whose red-hot breath, incredibly, cannot be extinguished by all the water in the sea.

The exploration of Lōʻihi is, I think, the greatest sea expedition in Hawaiʻi since Capt. James Cook dropped anchor in 1778.

We've been to the moon and back and still nobody knows the secrets of the deep.

Some scientists think underwater volcanoes might be the birthplace of life on earth.

An Australian researcher recently discovered fossilized remains of threadlike microbes that lived more than three billion years ago in a deep-sea volcano.

Makes you wonder what Madame Pele is really up to down there.

Divers in a mini-sub discovered that underwater earthquakes caused Pele's Dome to collapse last year, the *Star Bulletin* reported.

The collapse created a crater a half mile across and a thousand feet deep, into the heart of matter.

Sort of like nature's version of the Bikini nuclear explosion under the sea.

They renamed Pele's Dome Pele's Pit.

"This was a Mount St. Helens–sized volcanic event," said Alexander Malahoff, director of the Hawai'i Undersea Research Laboratory at the University of Hawai'i.

"What we learn from this event will have profound implications for virtually everything we now know about undersea volcanism."

The *Star Bulletin* went on to tell how two oceanographers in a Pisces IV mini-sub "skirted needlepoint pinnacles and towering peaks to explore Pele's Pit."

One scientist said, "It was like diving in Chicago through downtown high-rises."

The explorers entered the "forbidden pit," where the outside temperature was 410 degrees Fahrenheit, and dove into the abyss where they found—and here's the real story—strange new life forms.

Aliens.

"Six-inch-wide critters," the *Star Bulletin* said, quoting a scientist, "that look like mopheads. Several mopheads were collected."

Critters.

That's when I remembered the crewcut man with aquamarine eyes who got spooked when I asked about his "top secret" dives.

When I was a young, hotshot newspaperman in San Francisco, there would have been big, bold headlines in the *Chronicle*, saying: "Aliens Discovered in Pele's Pit."

Not today, at least not in Honolulu, where the Waikīkī premiere of *Lilo and Stritch,* a Disney cartoon about an alien that lands in Hawai'i, received more attention than the discovery of real alien life under the sea off the Big Island.

While I puzzled over the confused priorities and failure of attention, the *New York Times* reported on the 168th meeting of the American Association for the Advancement of Science in Boston. Geobiologists questioned the wisdom of bringing rocks back to earth from space. Or even dredging them up from the depths. They spoke of rocks as being "alive," teeming with life.

Alien life.

I know the University of Hawai'i scientists know better than to take rocks from Pele's Pit, but I wouldn't mind seeing one of those aliens they keep in a jar up at the university.

Or talking to the crewcut man with aquamarine eyes.

Grandma Brought Black Sand Home

Brad Smith

I must have been maybe ten or eleven when my grandfather died. My grandmother had finally talked my grandfather into going to Hawai'i on a vacation. She had gone before, and he had not, and, finally, they went together and, of course, they saw all the islands, did everything, the whole nine yards.

One of the things they wanted to see was the black sand beach on the Big Island of Hawai'i, which is no longer.

And, although she had been warned, my grandmother brought back black sand from that beach to the mainland. She said they had met some people on the beach who said you shouldn't bring back anything from the Big Island, at least not any volcanic rock. But it didn't seem like a big deal at the time, she said.

You know, it's real spooky, but within a year my grandfather died. My grandmother immediately took the black sand back to Hawai'i and left it there at the black sand beach.

It was, of course, after the fact. I do remember her many times telling us, "You know, you can't have that lava. I learned the hard way." That's her feeling, even now.

She told us about the black sand when I was in my teens; it just came up one day when we asked how Grandpa died. She feels that the reason my grandfather passed away is that she took the black sand.

I went to Hawai'i for the first time a few years ago. There was no black sand beach by the time I got there. It was all covered up by the lava flow. My grandmother now lives in Kona. She's in her eight-ies—I think she's eighty-eight now. She reiterated the story when we visited.

My sons wanted to take home a lava rock but, of course, my grandmother immediately intervened and retold the story about their great-grandfather's pass-ing. She's learned a lot more about Hawai'i's cus-toms, sacred places, *kapu*. So have we. You don't want to move rocks. Or sand.

When I go to Hawai'i, I never touch any rocks. Oh, I might pick one up and look at it, but I would-n't have any thought to take it back with me. No sir, not me. I get a little shudder even now when I think about it. It's still spooky, even though it happened so long ago.

Leave the Rocks Alone

Yu Shing Ting

A curse made up by a park ranger fifty-five years ago in an effort to stop visitors from collecting lava rocks is causing havoc over the power of these stones. Because of the superstitious belief that Madame Pele will inflict suffering on those who take her lava, the goddess of the volcano has been blamed for countless calamities.

That's why the staff at Hawai'i Volcanoes National Park doesn't want another story written about lava rocks. They say that each article generates even more returns of lava rocks to the park. Norrie Judd, one of the park's rangers, receives about five packages a day from visitors wanting to return something they took from the islands. A majority of the items sent back are lava rocks, but sand, coral, figurines and jewelry made out of lava are also common.

"People sent them back for a reason. They have very sad stories," she says. "Their house was broken into, they broke their leg, somebody died. Then they hear about this curse of taking things off the island and they send it back with their humble apology in hopes that the curse is broken."

Judd does not believe in Pele's Curse, and wishes people would stop sending the rocks back.

"We have not found any written curse in the history associated with lava rocks. It's very time-consuming to open the boxes and read the letters and put the rocks back," Judd complains.

In fact, it takes up so much of her time that she can no longer do it and has passed the job on to volunteers.

"Like any other national park in the country, it [Hawai'i Volcanoes] is protected by law, and you don't take things from it. And if everybody was just doing what they are supposed to be doing, we wouldn't be getting all these rocks," Judd says.

But for Patti Lee, a geology instructor at the University of Hawai'i, collecting lava rocks is part of her job. She hears the stories about people's misfortunes and the possible connection with Pele. In fact, she receives packages of lava rocks as well. And like Judd, she doesn't believe in the curse, but believes it's just a coincidence.

"They're looking for an excuse for their bad luck," she explains.

Lee collects her rocks from the Big Island, but not from Kīlauea. And in her thirteen years at UH, she says she has never experienced anything bad that she might blame on the rocks. Maybe it's because she uses them for educational purposes rather than for personal ones.

But there is one change she's noticed over the years: "The only thing that happens is that my husband's arms get longer and longer from bringing all these rocks home for me," Lee laughs.

Not everyone, however, agrees that the myth is just a hoax. Jon Osorio, a UH Hawaiian Studies professor, believes there is a possible link between people's bad experiences and Pele.

"For Hawaiians, there is a long tradition that you don't take things that don't belong to you," Osorio explains. "What it comes down to is a matter of respect."

Lava rocks are a *kinolau* (form) of Pele. And although some people see the *pōhaku* as just another rock, it is actually considered a valuable resource to Hawaiians.

"The rocks are there for the community," Osorio says. "To take them, you're stealing from the community."

And there are many phenomenal stories that have people thinking twice about stealing from Pele.

Crew members aboard a Hawaiian Airlines flight last year say that after takeoff, the pilot returned to the airport because of possible mechanical problems. While engineers examined the plane, a passenger handed over a lava rock to an airline employee. Engineers found nothing wrong with the plane, and the flight took off again—this time with no reason for the pilot to return.

Although nobody knows for sure if this incident was of Pele's doing, Osorio says he wouldn't be surprised if it was: "It's possible that there are lots of people taking lava rocks who have not had anything happen to them. In this particular case, that was probably Pele acting up, but what was so significant about this rock, I don't know."

On the other hand, musician Stephen Brown is positive about his encounter with Pele during his trip to the Big Island twenty-three years ago.

He came with his cousin who was moving to Kona. Their first stop was Hōnaunau, also known as the City of Refuge. While there, Brown picked up two perfect hula stones. Almost immediately strange things began to happen.

"First, the car overheated. Then my cousin's friend cut his foot while walking on some lava rocks," he remembers.

But that had no effect on Brown who, at their next stop, picked up a couple more rocks near the Kalapana lava flow to add to his collection. But this time, Pele made sure she would get his attention.

"All of a sudden, everything changed. My cousin and his girlfriend, who I have never seen argue, are at each other's throats. No one's enjoying themselves. My cousin's girlfriend takes off on her own and he chases after her. Then some guy comes and picks a fight with us at the car," Brown recalls. The two got back in the car and, after an unsuccessful search for the couple, they called it a night.

"It's about 2 a.m. and we decide to take the short-cut back to Kona. We're going up Saddle Road and there's a lot of turns and pretty much when the curves stop you're on top, between the two volcanoes," Brown remembers. "Then—right when it starts to straighten out—we see this figure of a person walking on the road. The person is not getting any closer as we're driving and we're thinking it's very strange. All of a sudden it looks like she's right in front of us and we screech [the brakes] and look. But we don't see her, and then we see her and then we don't see her. Next thing we know our car konks out."

After letting the car sit awhile, the two men successfully started the car again and, luckily, no more bizarre things happened. Brown returned home to Kuliou'ou the next day, but he did not yet escape the curse. The next morning he awoke very weak. He couldn't lift his arms or legs and had a hard time talking. His sister walked up to him and gave him a weird look.

"She grabs the mirror and there's, like, a golf-ball–sized lump on my neck," Brown explains.

Doctors at the hospital emergency room couldn't tell him what it was either. He called his mom on the Big Island.

"I told her something's wrong and the first thing she said was, 'What did you take from the Big Island?'"

She returned his rock collection, and once that happened—surprise!—the lump on Brown's neck disappeared. But he still bears a memory of Pele, a scar on his right hand from the fight with the stranger that eerie night in the car.

Whether Pele's Curse is real or not, there is one thing on which believers and nonbelievers both agree: Leave the rocks alone.

One Night in Pele's Garden of Woe

Rick Carroll

When the sun is at its zenith on the first Wednesday of each month, a time considered most auspicious in the Hawaiian calendar, a *kahu* on the Big Island of Hawai'i asks Madame Pele's permission to return yet another box of rocks to her Garden of Woe. That's what I call the newest landmark on the Kona Coast.

The garden, known locally as Ka Ahu Paepae o Hoaka Ho'omalu, is the final resting place for disturbed Hawaiian rocks. A disturbed Hawaiian rock, by definition, is one that has been taken from its original place in the Islands.

Every day boxes of disturbed rocks—*pōhaku* and *'ili'ili*—are returned to Hawai'i in the mail, always with a note of apology and a tale of woe.

For decades the rocks were sent to the home office of the Hawai'i Visitors Bureau in Waikīkī and forwarded to Hawai'i Volcanoes National Park rangers, who dutifully returned the rocks to Madame Pele's warm embrace.

Since all rocks in Hawai'i originate with Madame Pele, the fire goddess of the volcanoes, each rock is said to have *mana,* or supernatural power.

Some folks believe that if you take Madame Pele's rocks something awful will happen to you. The belief is widely known as Madame Pele's Curse.

Now, everyone in Hawai'i knows that's *shibai,* a story created by a Hilo tour guide in the 1940s to frighten tourists, but you can't convince the folks who send the rocks back. They believe the rocks caused them grief.

And so the rocks keep rolling in across the Pacific to end up here on a swale of black lava on the grounds of the Marriott Outrigger Waikoloa Beach Resort between the ancient fishponds of 'Anaeho'omalu and the Waikoloa petroglyph preserve.

The site of the rock repository was chosen because of its unusual geographic position in the archipelago. It sits at the *piko,* or navel, of the surrounding volcanic peaks of Haleakalā, Mauna Kea, Mauna Loa, Kohala, and Hualālai.

Only the peak of Kīlauea Volcano, where Madame Pele's been dancing on the East Rift Zone since 1983, is out of sight, although her smoky breath darkens the sky on Kona days when the air is still.

❖

To this almost sacred place, for the last three years it has been my good fortune to be invited on

Halloween to tell true, first-person tales from my six spooky books.

Usually, I tell spooky stories in gathering darkness under rustling palm trees on the black lava seacoast. This time Noelani Whittington, in an obvious attempt to test my nerve, asked the hotel staff to set up lawn chairs next to the new rock garden.

I decided to take a look at this new venue and found a pile of red and black volcanic rocks, some smooth as glass, others porous as a sponge. Each rock represented trouble for some sorry wretch.

I tried to guess which rock caused a Douglas fir tree to crush a Puyallup bungalow, a head-on Porsche crash in La Mesa, a slip-and-fall in a Kennebunkport bathtub, and the premature death of a Primadonna cocktail waitress in Reno.

All the rocks looked innocent, the sort of stones anyone might pick up and take home as a souvenir of Hawai'i. The power of these rocks, it appeared, had been spent.

After sunset—in what passes for a dark and stormy night in Hawai'i—nearly one hundred souls huddled together under flickering tiki torches while a hard wind swept down from Mauna Kea's summit.

I pointed out the rock garden and told how rocks are considered special in Hawai'i, how they have spiritual power, and that the rocks they saw here had all been returned to Hawai'i by unfortunate souls who claim they fell victim to Pele's Curse.

Everyone looked at the rocks. Some gave a little shudder. Tell you more about the rocks later, I said.

I then told true stories about night marchers who follow trails on the Kona Coast, of pressing spirits who hold you captive in your bed, of old bones and stones and things that go bump in the night.

Soon everyone was holding their elbows, shivering in the tropic night, experiencing that delightful spine-tingling sensation folks in Hawai'i call chicken skin.

I told Nanette Napoleon's "Old Hawaiian Graveyards," Dr. Phil Helfrich's "Limu Make O Hāna," and Dominic Kealoha Aki's "The Night Madame Pele Visited Hanauma Bay."

I told how the wrong body ended up in a casket at a Lāna'i funeral and how the skeleton of an old fisherman caused migraine headaches in Waimea.

Everyone wanted to hear more Pele stories. One man wanted to know "the real story" about Pele's rocks.

"First, you need to know the truth: the story of Pele's Curse is a fiction, invented by a Hawai'i tour guide here on the Big Island. The story has no basis in fact in Hawai'i legend. That is true.

"And this is true: bad things often happen to people who take Pele's rocks. Some people lose their jobs or their homes, have terrible accidents, end up in the hospital, die. The rocks you see here were returned by those unlucky folks.

"So, now, we have two opposing truths, and in the end, it is up to you to decide what to believe.

"I've got a great idea," I said. "To prove Madame Pele's Curse, true or false, let's get up, go over to the rocks, pick one up, and take it home.

"Keep it for a year, until next Halloween, then let me know what, if anything, happened to you. Okay, let's all go get a rock."

Everyone laughed nervously. Nobody moved.

"What's the matter?" I asked.

"I just told you Madame Pele's Curse isn't true. Nothing will happen to you. C'mon, let's all get a rock."

Nobody moved.

"I don't believe this," I said, grinning. "All of you believe in a story made up by a tour guide?"

Everybody giggled. Nobody moved.

"Okay, here's an easier way to test the veracity of Madame Pele's Curse. Let's all go get a rock and take it to our room. Keep it overnight. Put it back in the morning. Just let me know how you slept. Okay?"

Nobody moved.

"What's the matter?" I asked. "You don't believe me?"

A hand shot up from the back row.

"You shoulda been a lawyer," a fellow said.

Everyone had a good laugh.

Nobody took a rock home that night.

Related Reading

Books:

Barnard, Walther, ed. *Mauna Loa—A Source Book: Historical Eruptions and Exploration.* Vol. 3, *The Post Jaggar Years (1940–1991).* Department of Geosciences, SUNY College at Fredonia, NY, 1980.

Bevens, Darcy, ed. *On The Rim of Kilauea: Excerpts from the Volcano House Register, 1865–1955.* Hawai'i National Park: Hawai'i Natural History Association, 1992.

Blickhahn, Harry Miller. *Uncle George of Kilauea: The Story of George Lycurgus.* Volcano House, 1961.

Castro, Nash. *The Land of Pele: A Historical Sketch of Hawaii National Park.* Hawai'i National Park: Hawai'i Natural History Association, 1953.

Ching, Linda. *Hawaiian Goddesses.* Commemorative ed. Honolulu: Hawaiian Goddesses Publishing Co., 1987.

Ellis, William. *Journal of William Ellis: Narrative of a Tour of Hawaii, Or Owhyhee; With Remarks on the History, Traditions, Manner, Customs, and Language of the Inhabitants of the Sandwich Islands.* 1825. Reprint, Rutland, Vermont: Charles E. Tuttle Co., 1979.

Emerson, Nathaniel B. *Pele and Hiʻiaka: A Myth From Hawaii*. Tokyo: Charles E. Tuttle Co., Inc., 1978.

Frierson, Pamela. *The Burning Island: A Journey Through Myth and History in Volcano Country, Hawaii*. San Francisco: Sierra Club Books, 1991.

Gutmanis, June. Na Pule Kahiko*: Ancient Hawaiian Prayers*. Honolulu: Editions Limited, 1983.

Hongo, Garrett K. *Volcano: A Memoir of Hawaii*. New York: Alfred A. Knopf Inc., 1995.

Nimmo, H. Arlo. *The Pele Literature: An Annotated Bibliography of the English Language Literature on Pele, Volcano Goddess of Hawaii*. Honolulu: Bishop Museum Press, 1992.

Westervelt, William D., comp. and trans. *Hawaiian Legends of Volcanoes*. Rutland, Vermont: Charles E. Tuttle Co., 1976.

Articles:

Apple, Russ. "Tales of Old Hawaii." *Honolulu Star-Bulletin* columns, 1969–1980.

Ashdown, Inez. "Pele Calls on Maui." *Honolulu Star-Bulletin,* June 6, 1950, p. 19. Reprinted in *Mauna Loa—A Source Book*, p. 134.

"Calling Madame Pele," *Honolulu Star Bulletin,* March 29, 1984, sec. A, p. 8. Reprinted in *Mauna Loa—A Source Book,* p. 233.

Engledow, Ed. "Return of the Phantom Dog," *Honolulu Star-Bulletin,* May 18, 1961, p. 1. Reprinted in *Mauna Loa—A Source Book,* p. 289.

Takeuchi, Floyd K., and Jan TenBruggencate. "It's a Bird, It's a Plane, It's Pele." *Honolulu Star-Bulletin and Advertiser,* April 1, 1984, sec. A, p. 1. Reprinted in *Mauna Loa—A Source Book,* p. 237.

Contributors

Dominic Aki is the owner/operator of Mauka Makai Ecotours, a Hawaiian cultural ecotour company. www.oahu-ecotours.com. His story "The Night Pele Visited Hanauma Bay" first appeared in *Hawai'i's Best Spooky Tales 4* (Bess Press, 2000).

Kalina Chang, a resident of Kahalu'u, O'ahu, is married and has two sons and a daughter. She does crafts, graphic art, and freelance writing, and paddles with Keahiakahoe Canoe Club. She lived in the Waihe'e Valley for ten years, during which she had many encounters with the supernatural. Her story "A Lady's Advice" first appeared in *Hawai'i's Best Spooky Tales 5* (Bess Press, 2001), as did her stories "*Kolohe* Spirits" and "Drums in the Night."

Julieta P. Cobb lives in Honolulu.

Michael Dalke is a designer of tropical-style homes and furnishings in Hawai'i and the Pacific. He's created furniture for Pier One, designed Beverly Hills boutiques and Las Vegas casinos. Two decades ago Dalke came to Hawai'i and began exploring appropriate shelter for the tropics. He pioneered the use of *bangkiri*, a termite-proof Indonesian hardwood that resembles teak. His work includes houses in Lanikai, Waikāne, the Big Island of Hawai'i, Kaua'i, and resorts in the far Pacific. He lives in Bali. His story "No Sleep in Pele's World" first appeared in *Hawai'i's Best Spooky Tales 5* (Bess Press, 2001). www.tropicstructures.com

Elise (Pua Lilia) DuFour lives in San Francisco, where she works with transformational specialists helping others transform their lives and attain their dreams. If she's not in, on, around, over, or under the water, you'll find her exploring the coast, wine country, Yosemite, and the city with camera in tow, looking for treasures. Her story "Pele Dream" first appeared in *Hawai'i's Best Spooky Tales 4* (Bess Press, 2000).

Of Native Hawaiian and Asian ancestry, **Nyla Fujii-Babb** has been a professional storyteller, actress, and librarian in Hawai'i for twenty-five years. Her story "At the Volcano's Edge" first appeared in *Hawai'i's Best Spooky Tales 2* (Bess Press, 1998).

David Hallsted is joyfully wed to Susan Wittstock. They have two boys, Jon and Ben. They all live in the sea-breezed hills of Berkeley, California. Susan and David have vacationed in Hawai'i for their honeymoon and their tenth anniversary. Next trip they plan to bring the kids. David is a closet psychic who would rather get a job involving the psychic world than inspect widgets for a living. "And no," he says, "I don't do readings. Mind you, I can talk with everything and anything out there, but try to get a paying job doing that. Thus . . . good widget . . . good widget . . . good widget . . . bad widget [toss over head] . . . good widget...good widget."

Fox Harmon lives in Honolulu with her three children and their cat, Nefertiti. Her story "The Dark Mirror" appeared in *Hawai'i's Best Spooky Tales 5* (Bess Press, 2001). The mirror, inherited from her dearly departed Filipino grandmother, who enjoyed clairvoyant powers, is on view at Prosperity Corner in Kaimukī, where everyone can encounter the different characters who now and then surface.

Dwynn Leialoha Kamai, daughter of Heine and Winona Kamai, was born and raised in Pālolo Valley, O'ahu. She is employed by Bank of Hawaii as a branch concierge and is a crafter of etched glass.

Geophysicist **Bernard G. Mendonca** joined the Mauna Loa observatory as a part-time government employee in 1958 while a University of Hawai'i student. He originally helped the U.S. Weather Bureau process analysis from atmospheric monitoring of solar radiation and later, in a classified program, monitored nuclear radiation for the Atomic Energy

Commission. He now works at Geophysical Monitoring for Climatic Change in Boulder, Colorado. His account of "The White Dog of Mauna Loa" originally appeared in *Mauna Loa—A Source Book: Historical Eruptions and Exploration,* Vol. 3, *The Post-Jaggar Years (1940–1991),* edited by Walther M. Bernard, Dept. of Geosciences, State University of New York College at Fredonia, New York. His story "The White Dog of Mauna Loa" first appeared in *Hawai'i's Best Spooky Tales: The Original* (Bess Press, 1996).

Hawai'i-born author and former *Honolulu Advertiser* reporter **Gordon Morse** lives in Volcano, the village near the entrance to Hawai'i Volcanoes National Park, home of Madame Pele. His story "Pele" first appeared in *Hawai'i's Best Spooky Tales* (Bess Press, 1997). His story "Cliffside Burial Caves of Waipi'o Valley" appeared in *Hawai'i's Best Spooky Tales: The Original* (Bess Press, 1996).

Lani T. Paiva is a judicial clerk supervisor for the Family and Probation Services, Third Circuit Court, in Hilo, Hawai'i. She is married and has two children. Her story "Lady in Red" first appeared in *Hawai'i's Best Spooky Tales* (Bess Press, 1997).

Brad Smith lives on San Juan Island in the Puget Sound and frequently visits the Big Island of Hawai'i with his wife and two sons. They don't collect rocks. His story "Grandma Brought Black Sand Home" first appeared in *Hawai'i's Best Spooky Tales 4* (Bess Press, 2000).

David Soares was born in Honolulu. Retired from Chevron USA, he is active in the St. Louis Alumni Association and Notre Dame Alumni Club of Hawai'i.

Russell Stevens is a retired lawyer and former attorney general of Guam who now lives in San Diego, California. His books include *Guam, Birth of a Territory* (two editions).

Dr. Michael Kekahimoku Sturrock, a 1964 graduate of Kamehameha School for Boys, currently lives in Bellevue, Washington, where he is a veterinarian in private practice. His family originates from Kohala, Hawai'i, and he spent his boyhood summers in Waimea, where he learned to appreciate the power of Pele. His story "A *Pilialoha* with Pele" first appeared in *Hawai'i's Best Spooky Tales 3* (Bess Press, 1999).

Mike Sunnafrank is Professor of Communication and Director of Study Abroad at the University of Minnesota Duluth. Each winter break he brings students to Hawai'i to learn about Native Hawaiian history and culture as well as to learn about the current issues facing Hawaiians and other local communities. He first visited Hawai'i in the mid-1960s as a guest of several Farrington graduates he played football with in California. His wife, Donna, is a Leilehua graduate.

Barbara Swift came to Hawai'i nearly forty years ago from Manhattan Beach, California. She married local boy Llewellyn Swift thirty-six years ago, and they have two daughters. For the past twenty-nine years, Barbara has owned and operated Aunty Barbara's Day Care. The little girl in the story, daughter number two, is now twenty-five, is married, and has a child of her own.

Ted Timboy was born in Honolulu but grew up on a coffee farm in Kona (Captain Cook). He grew up hearing spooky stories from his father and grandmother. He attended UH-Mānoa before moving to California in 1985. A frequent traveler (Europe five times, Australia once), in the past few years he has felt a strong desire and need to return home to Hawai'i.

Yu Shing Ting is a senior staff writer for *MidWeek*, where this article first appeared. Born in Hong Kong, she moved to Hawai'i with her family at age two. She grew up in Hawai'i Kai and currently lives in Mānoa. Yu Shing is a journalism graduate of the University of Hawai'i, and enjoys running, surfing, playing basketball, and dancing hula. Her story

"Leave the Rocks Alone" first appeared in *MidWeek* and also appeared in *Hawai'i's Best Spooky Tales 5* (Bess Press, 2001).

Walt Wrzesniewski was born in Philadelphia and reborn in Hawai'i. He and Janine, his wife, live in Kahalu'u, where they appreciate the *'āina,* their growing *'ohana,* and music.

Cheryl Zimbra, a lifelong resident of Windward O'ahu, enjoys spending time with her two dogs, family, and friends. Her hobbies include writing poetry and playing darts. Her story "The Hitchhiker of Laupāhoehoe" first appeared in *Hawai'i's Best Spooky Tales 5* (Bess Press, 2001).

About Rick Carroll

Rick Carroll is the author of many books about Hawai'i, including six titles in the best-selling Hawai'i's Best Spooky Tales series. He is also the host of the award-winning Hawai'i 's Best Spooky Tales Festival, held each year in Waikīkī at the Outrigger Hotel.

A former daily journalist with the *San Francisco Chronicle*, Carroll covered Hawai'i and the Pacific as a special correspondent for United Press International. He won a National Headliners Award for his reporting from the Philippines during the final days of the Marcos era.

As a travel writer, he received the Lowell Thomas Award of the Society of American Travel Writers for "The Eyes of Easter Island," which appeared in the *San Francisco Chronicle*. He also received the Gold Award of the Pacific Asia Travel Association for his illustrated reports from French Polynesia.

With his wife, Marcie Carroll, he edited *Hawai'i: True Stories of the Island Spirit* (Travelers' Tales, 1999) which critics called "the best example of contemporary Hawai'i nonfiction." Their other books in national release include *The Unofficial Guide to Hawaii* (John Wiley and Sons, 2002) and *The Unofficial Guide to Maui* (John Wiley and Sons, 2003).

His next book, "Huahine, Island of the Lost Canoe," is a true-life archaeological mystery about the only relic Polynesian voyaging canoe ever found.

He is now writing the biography of the late Hawaiian singer Israel Kamakawiwo'ole.

He lives on a night marcher's trail on Windward O'ahu, and near Cape Fear in the Outer Banks of North Carolina.